Rolf H. Weber

Principles for governing the Internet

A comparative analysis

Published in 2015 by the United Nations Educational, Scientific and Cultural Organization
7, place de Fontenoy, 75352 Paris 07 SP, France

© UNESCO 2015
ISBN 978-92-3-100125-3

This publication is available in Open Access under the Attribution-ShareAlike 3.0 IGO (CC-BY-SA 3.0 IGO) license (http://creativecommons.org/licenses/by-sa/3.0/igo/). By using the content of this publication, the users accept to be bound by the terms of use of the UNESCO Open Access Repository (http://www.unesco.org/open-access/terms-use-ccbysa-en).

The designations employed and the presentation of material throughout this publication do not imply the expression of any opinion whatsoever on the part of UNESCO concerning the legal status of any country, territory, city or area or of its authorities, or concerning the delimitation of its frontiers or boundaries.

The ideas and opinions expressed in this publication are those of the authors; they are not necessarily those of UNESCO and do not commit the Organization.

Cover illustration: © Shutterstock/greiss design

Typeset and printed by UNESCO
Printed in France

Table of Contents

Foreword 5

Executive Summary 7

1. **Introduction** 9

2. **Methodology** 13

2.1 Initial Background 13

2.2 Concepts Based on Indicators 14

2.3 Concept Based on Layers 15

2.4 Concept Based on Substantive Objectives 16

2.5 Accountability Mechanisms in Particular 21

2.6 Theoretical Framework for the Analysis of the Documents 22

3. **Analysis of Documents** 23

3.1 General Observations of the Historical, Political, Economic, and Social Background of the Documents dealing with Internet Governance Principles 23
    3.1.1 Overview 23
    3.1.2 Short Description of the Available Internet Governance Principles 24
    3.1.3 Conclusion 33

3.2 Access and Openness 34
    3.2.1 Access 34
        3.2.1.1 Contents of Documents 34
        3.2.1.2 Conclusion 38
    3.2.2 Openness 38
        3.2.2.1 Contents of Documents 38
        3.2.2.2 Conclusion 41

3.3 Freedom of Expression 41
    3.3.1 Contents of Documents 41
    3.3.2 Conclusion 47

3.4 Privacy 47
    3.4.1 Contents of Documents 47
    3.4.2 Conclusion 53

3.5	Ethics		54
	3.5.1	Contents of Documents	54
	3.5.2	Conclusion	57
3.6	Multistakeholder Participation		57
	3.6.1	Contents of Documents	57
	3.6.2	Conclusion	64
3.7	Gender Equality		64
	3.7.1	Contents of Documents	64
	3.7.2	Conclusion	68
3.8	Sustainable Development		68
	3.8.1	Contents of Documents	68
	3.8.2	Conclusion	71
3.9	Issues of Culture, Science and the Social and Human Sciences, and Education		71
	3.9.1	Cultural Diversity	71
	3.9.2	Science	73
	3.9.3	Education	73
4.	**Relevance for UNESCO**		**75**
4.1	Findings of the Documents' Analysis		75
	4.1.1	Compatibility and Completeness of Existing Documents	75
	4.1.2	Normative character of existing documents	77
	4.1.3	Accountability mechanisms	78
4.2	Salient Issues for UNESCO		80
5.	**Conclusions**		**81**
6.	**References**		**83**
Appendix			**84**
Internet Universality: A Means Towards Building Knowledge Societies and the Post-2015 Sustainable Development Agenda			84
1.	Why a concept of "Internet Universality"?		85
2.	Unpacking the concept of "Internet Universality"		86
3.	How the concept of "Internet Universality" is relevant to UNESCO		88
4.	Conclusion		88

Foreword

By Resolution 52 of the 37th General Conference in 2013, UNESCO was mandated to conduct a comprehensive and consultative study on Internet-related issues.

The consultation that ensued revealed strong interest from Member States for information about the existing Internet-related principles in other fora, which could help inform the Organization's governing bodies when deciding on future actions for UNESCO.

As a result, this research was commissioned. It identified more than 50 Internet-specific declarations and frameworks relevant to Internet principles. While previous analyses of these documents provided important context for UNESCO's Internet Study, it was also clear that there a need for a specific review from the perspective of UNESCO's mandate.

UNESCO expresses its thanks to Rolf Weber who have delivered this comprehensive and detailed assessment. UNESCO also thanks 16 international experts who have kindly reviewed the draft and provided their valuable inputs.

The findings of this research have contributed to the final Internet study, which has been published as Keystones to foster inclusive Knowledge Societies: Access to information and knowledge, Freedom of Expression, Privacy, and Ethics on a Global Internet.

The findings were also part of UNESCO's Connecting the Dots Conference held in March 2015, and we have pleasure in publishing them now as the fifth in the UNESCO Series on Internet Freedom.

A key backdrop for this research is the World Summit on the Information Society (WSIS) and its follow-up. For UNESCO, this means promoting progress towards inclusive knowledge societies. We have developed the draft concept of "Internet Universality", based on accepted UNESCO positions, to identify to how the Internet could help achieve knowledge societies.

Accordingly, Internet Universality highlights the contribution that can be made by an Internet that is based on the universal norms of being: human Rights-based; Open; Accessible to all; and with Multi-stakeholder participation (summarized in the acronym R.O.A.M.). This draft concept has relevance to the Organization's work in many areas – including online freedom of expression and privacy; efforts to advance universality in education, social inclusion and gender equality; multilingualism in cyberspace; access to information and knowledge; and ethical dimensions of information society.

Against this background, the analysis in this publication has also assessed the subject matter in relation to the Internet Universality concept and the R.O.A.M framework. In addition, it examined the range of documents from the point of view of UNESCO concerns such as the Priority Gender Equality, Priority Africa, sustainable development, the Decade for the Rapprochement of Cultures, and other UNESCO concerns.

The outcome of the review shows that none of the existing external statements fully meet UNESCO's interests and mandate. It proposes therefore that UNESCO adopt the concept of "Internet Universality" and R.O.A.M framework as the Organization's own clear identifier for approaching the various fields of Internet issues and their intersections with UNESCO concerns.

Through past research, UNESCO has succeeded in raising awareness and promoting good practice in our Series on Internet Freedom: *Freedom of connection, freedom of expression: the changing legal and regulatory ecology shaping the Internet (2011), Global survey on Internet Privacy and Freedom of Expression (2012), Fostering freedom online: the role of Internet intermediaries (2014), and Building digital safety for journalism: a survey of selected issues (2015)*.

We believe that the rich material in current study will be of great value to UNESCO Member States, industry actors, the technical community, Intergovernmental organizations, private sector, civil society, and others both national and international. In this way, the publication can make a contribution to advancing our understanding of knowledge societies.

Getachew Engida

Deputy Director-General of UNESCO

Executive Summary

The existing regulatory framework of the Internet, respectively, is composed of different national laws, self-regulatory guidelines and a number of multilateral treaties having relevance in varying degrees. In this fluid and distributed area, the evolution of applicable overall substance principles can play an important role. These principles should be developed by governments, the private sector, civil society, and academia, together in their respective roles; norms, rules, and decision-making procedures based on consensus can help to shape an optimum design and use of the Internet.

UNESCO has been involved in the development of Internet Governance principles mainly through its «Internet Universality» concept, encompassing four key pillars, namely Rights, Openness, Accessibility, and Multistakeholder Participation (called R.O.A.M.). To assist in strengthening the role of UNESCO in this field, this study provides a comprehensive overview of the core documents about Internet Governance principles developed and adopted by various other stakeholders. Areas of similarities, overlaps, consensus, differences, and disagreements have been identified by using comparative indicators which reflect UNESCO's initiatives on (i) access to information and knowledge, (ii) freedom of expression, (iii) privacy, and (iv) ethical dimensions of the information society as well as UNESCO's five programme areas. The analyzed documents are put into the historical, political, economic and social context, assessed in view of a potential normative use as well as accountability, and evaluated in respect of their compatibility and completeness in light of UNESCO's mandate and positions.

This study encompasses both quantitative and qualitative assessment: On the one hand, the more than 50 evaluated declarations, guidelines, and frameworks are briefly described in the given context; on the other hand, the issues contained in these documents are also qualitatively analyzed. In this, it is evident that multiple initiatives have been taken during the last 25 years. The prevailing impression is of a wide diversity of documents and of attention to diverse Internet Governance principles. The contents of the analyzed documents heavily depend on the given actors and environment at the time of the drafting. Furthermore, some principles (for example freedom of expression, access to information, privacy) have gained much more attention than other principles (for example, multistakeholder participation, ethical behavior, sustainability, education, gender equality).

While the normative character of the documents containing Internet Governance principles complements much of the mandate and work of UNESCO, there is no existing external document covering all concerns of the Organization. Due to its cross-sectoral character, UNESCO is particularly well placed to advance universality in social inclusion, education, multilingualism, ethical behavior, and gender equality. This is why the «Internet Universality» concept and the R.O.A.M. framework with the four key principles can be well linked to the general objectives of UNESCO, i.e. to communication and information issues, education, social and human science as well as sustainable development (including priority for Africa). UNESCO's already developed principles can become a clear identifier of the Organization's way of approaching the various fields of Internet issues.

As the «Internet Universality» concept and its principles are all at a general level, consensus on their relevance to UNESCO's priorities might be achievable. Due to its broad reach, UNESCO is also well placed to further develop indicators for the R.O.A.M. framework. An example of indicators could be those for a successful multistakeholder process, clarifying how meaningful participation is achieved and how stakeholders can reach the desired level of inclusiveness. Thereby, multistakeholderism could potentially overcome the real and threatened conflicts that might fragment the Internet. The quality of multistakeholderism is essential for the effectiveness and sustainability of Internet Governance.

If the normative and programmatic efforts of UNESCO are reinforced as outlined in this study and if the «Internet Universality» concept becomes more operational, as elaborated in the full analysis, then policy development can be enriched. In this way, UNESCO can contribute to a universal Internet that brings the sum of its Member States closer to being «Knowledge Societies».

1. Introduction[*]

Cyberspace encompasses technological, social, cultural, economic, and legal facets. The existing regulatory framework is composed of different national laws, manifold selfregulatory guidelines and a number of multilateral treaties that have relevance in varying degrees. In this fluid and distributed arena, the evolution of applicable overall principles can play a valuable role.[1]

Discussions on this subject are variously described under the broad label of "Internet Governance", applied as an inclusive reference for the ongoing set of disputes and deliberations over how the Internet is used, coordinated, managed and shaped.[2] From the World Summit on the Information Society, the following definition emerged: "…Internet governance is the development and application by governments, the private sector and civil society, in their respective roles, of shared principles, norms, rules, decision-making procedures, and programmes that shape the evolution and use of the Internet."[3]

A large number of Internet Governance declarations, guidelines, and frameworks have been produced and reviewing these documents is the core purpose of this study. The review takes place against the backdrop of UNESCO as an important player in discussions about principles relevant to Internet Governance. Although UNESCO does not have a specific mandate covering the full field of Internet Governance as such, areas of its work have significant bearing on aspects of the subject, and vice versa. One element highlighting the intersection has been the exploration at UNESCO, starting in September 2013, of the "Internet Universality" framework. This concept summarizes the significance of relevant principles that have been agreed in various decisions by the UNESCO Member States. In particular, "Internet Universality" is constituted by four key principles: Rights, Openness, Accessibility, and Multistakeholder Participation (summarized in the acronym R.O.A.M).[4] How these articulate to the numerous relevant statements by other actors is analysed throughout the pages that follow.

The roots of the research presented in this current publication lie in UNESCO's fulfilment of Resolution 52 of its 37th General Conference in November 2013, as agreed by the Organization's 195 Member States. This resolution called for a comprehensive and consultative multistakeholder study, within the mandate of UNESCO, on Internet-related issues of access to information and knowledge, freedom of expression, privacy, and the ethical dimensions of the Information Society. The methodology of such a wide-ranging study included consultative meetings with Member States and other actors, where it was motivated that UNESCO's research should be located within an analysis of the wider picture of existing statements about the Internet, so as to avoid duplication or mission-creep. As a result this publication was commissioned as a feeder document for the wider study, and it also stands alone as a review of more than 50 statements that are pertinent to many of the issues within Internet Governance. This research is referenced within the wider study,

---

[*] The author would like to thank the UNESCO Secretariat for their highly appreciated support. Valuable inputs to an earlier draft of the study have been given by Eduardo Bertoni, Anriette Esterhuysen, Marianne Franklin, Grace Githaiga, Wolfgang Kleinwächter, and Stefaan Verhulst. For the research work I am very grateful to my University assistant Ulrike I. Heinrich, Attorney-at-Law, who has actively promoted the project.
[1] Weber, 2014.
[2] Mueller, 2010, 9; DeNardis, 2014, 6.
[3] WSIS, 2005
[4] See http://www.unesco.org/new/fileadmin/MULTIMEDIA/HQ/CI/CI/pdf/news/internet_universality_en.pdf.

providing context which informs the particular niche and value-add for UNESCO's possible future options on Internet-related issues within its mandate.

Against this backdrop, some observations can be made about the overall field of Internet Governance within which numerous positions have been expressed. Five major features of global Internet Governance have been identified by scholars, all of which are potentially impacted upon by overarching principles:[5]

(1) *Arrangements of technical architecture as arrangements of power*: Internet protocols and standards are also political in both their design and effects; therefore, Internet Governance decisions involve both scientific reasoning and social considerations of power and authority, including policies about how the technical architectures are used to regulate and control content. This architecture relates to the principle of "Openness" in the "Internet Universality" concept, and is particularly relevant to issues such as open standards, open access/architecture, open knowledge resources, and open innovation, as well as relevant to issues around entry barriers (whether state imposed or privately enforced).

(2) *Internet infrastructure as proxy for content control:* Internet policies such as deeppacket inspection are being used for content mediation functions for which they were not originally designed. Such applications of political and economic power raise questions of democratic mandate and oversight. Furthermore, the same technologies that improve citizen information diffusion are applied by many actors to filter and censor information as well as creating systems of surveillance. These approaches impact on the exercise of human rights (such as the freedom of expression and privacy) as well as the net neutrality principle as part of "Openness" which are substantive pillars of UNESCO's "Universality Concept".

(3) *Public-private issues in Internet Governance*: Important Internet Governance mechanisms such as the domain name system are mainly governed and shaped by privatesector and technical actors (also called "privatization"). The assumption of functions for the public good by these actors has in the past contributed to the success of new technological networks. At the same time, there are debates about the appropriate role of other actors (eg. states, interstate organisations, civil society, academia, etc). The fourth pillar of UNESCO's "Universality Concept" refers to multistakeholder participation, which entails a wide spread of participatory decision-making while allowing that different formulae may be appropriate for different issues.

(4) *Internet control points as sites of global conflict over competing values*: Control points on the Internet include amongst others Critical Internet Resources (like Internet addresses), protocols and interconnection regimes. Besides how these issues implicate human rights, there is also the question as to users' ability to participate in issues of values and ethics on the Internet. In turn, this depends on Internet access as a social dimension. These elements are foreseen in the third pillar of the "Internet Universality" concept, which highlights universal access, multilingualism, quality of content, user empowerment and ethical considerations.

(5) *Regional geopolitics versus collective action problems of Internet globalization*: Notwithstanding the internationalization of many activities, it cannot be overlooked that global Internet stability is also dependent on local Internet conditions since local oversight and local infrastructure bottlenecks can serve as "obligatory passage points" for international traffic.[6] National and regional initiatives addressing geopolitical strategies need to be

---

5 For further details see DeNardis, 2014, 7-18.
6 De Nardis, 2014, 217.

balanced against global collective actions in regard to the impact on the transnational Internet. These political influences are not directly addressed in the "Universality Concept", but are partly reflected in the issue of "Rights", for example in cultural diversity (which also accords with "Openness" in the sense of diverse interpretations that nevertheless remain consistent with the broad framework of human rights).

For UNESCO's activities that impact on Internet policies, and vice versa, additional research on Internet Governance principles (declarations, normative frameworks and accountability measures) is of relevance; therefore, this comprehensive study attempts to achieve the following objectives:

- to provide a comprehensive review of the core principles in key initiatives on Internet Governance principles which have been developed and adopted by various stakeholders, identifying areas of similarities, overlaps, consensus, differences and disagreements, thereby using comparative indicators; these initiatives should be of relevance to the four fields of UNESCO's Internet Study (UNESCO 2015[7]), i.e. (i) access to information and knowledge, (ii) freedom of expression, (iii) privacy and (iv) ethical dimensions of the information society; they should also be of relevance to UNESCO priorities and themes, and to UNESCO's five programme areas;

- to put these texts into the historical, political, economic and social context, and to analyze the extent to which various declarations have been used as normative instruments, with reference to related accountability mechanisms and indicators;

- to analyze the compatibility and completeness of existing documents with respect to UNESCO's mandate and positions, as encompassed by the draft concept of "Internet Universality" (IU) and the R.O.A.M. framework (meaning four principles of IU: Human Rights based, Openness, Accessible for all and Multistakeholder participation), and to identify any gaps;

- to provide elements for a user-friendly online resource web page to Member States, civil society, the private sector, technical community and individuals with open access to the documents and data visualization;

- to clarify elements that are relevant to UNESCO actions, for consideration by Member States, based on a thorough understanding of existing declarations, frameworks and accountability mechanisms.

In pursuit of these objectives and in concretizing the general foundation of the research work, the key questions of the following study can be phrased as follows:

- What has been developed and adopted by stakeholders as regards international and regional declarations, guidelines, frameworks, and accountability mechanisms related to one or more fields of the UNESCO study?

- What were the historical, political, economic, and social contexts that led to the documents' creation and have the documents been used as normative instruments by the stakeholders?

- In particular, what specific options concerning Internet principles might UNESCO Member States consider, including their relevance for the Organization's Global

---

7   http://www.unesco.org/new/en/internetstudy

Priorities of Africa and Gender Equality, shaping the post-2015 development agenda, supporting the goals of Small Island Developing States and taking forward the Decade for the Rapprochement of Cultures?

- Is there a gap that needs to be filled to cover the areas under UNESCO's mandate?

- How does UNESCO's draft concept of "Internet Universality" compare with the existing declarations and frameworks? How could the concept be measured and applied?

In terms of limitations, the following study did not collect all available Internet Governance principles documents,[8] but focused on those with an acceptable degree of finalization and with a view to assessing substantive gaps rather than mapping each and every statement.[9]

The main focus throughout is to put attention on foundational Internet Governance principles even if more extensive wording or even documents would be available. For example, the study analyzes the 10 principles of the Internet Rights and Principles Dynamic Coalition (IRPC) not the full Charter[10] even if some of its 21 Articles are relevant for this survey. At the same time, the online resource that accompanies this study does provide a more extensive mapping, which is a knowledge resource that can complement the sample of materials analyzed here.[11]

Further, it is acknowledged that not all documents that mention a given concept apply exactly the same meaning to it. However, as an indicative process, the review in this study is still able to generate insight into the patterns of convergences, divergences and gaps.[12]

The study analyzes its selection of documents with a methodology of specific indicators designed in relation to the "Internet Universality" concept. The applied research encompasses a quantitative and a qualitative assessment: On the one hand, the existing declarations, guidelines, and frameworks are listed and the contents are quantitatively linked to the relevant UNESCO objectives; on the other hand, the issues contained in these documents are qualitatively analyzed.

---

8   This report examines declarations, guidelines, and frameworks and not indirectly binding legal instruments such as international treaties, regulations and directives of the European Union, and national law. Documents such as questionnaires will not be assessed.

9   For example, the study does not consider the Preliminary Declaration of the Digital Human Rights of the Forum D'Avignon (http://www.ddhn.org/index-en.php), or the evolving proposals for a Magna Carta for the Internet by Tim Berners-Lee (https://webwewant.org/). Nor did it examine issue specific principles such as the Global Privacy Standards (2006) and the "Madrid Resolution" (2009) of the International Data Protection and Privacy Commissioners Conference, or the OECD Privacy Principles. It was also not possible during the time period to review in detail documents such as "An Internet for the Common Good: Engagement, Empowerment and Justice for All" (2013). A number of historical documents such as that of the MacBride Report of 1980 or the Communication Rights for the Information Society have also not been covered. Individual items such as submissions to the Netmundial Summit (2014) have not been analysed, although the Netmundial statement itself is in- cluded. The Feminist Principles for the Internet, produced by the Association for Progressive Communications, are considered in this study specifically in relation to the focused issue of gender. Also not included are statementsn from the Freedom Online Coalition conferences, the Global Network Initiative, or the UN or Organisation of American States Special Rapporteurs.

10 Internet Rights and Principles Coalition, The Charter of Human Rights and Principles for the Internet, 4th ed. of August 2014, http://internetrightsandprinciples.org/site/wp-content/uploads/2014/08/IRPC_Booklet-English_4thedition.pdf.

11 http://www.unesco.org/new/en/communication-and-information/events/calendar-of-events/events-websites/connecting-the-dots/the-study/international-and-regional-instruments/.

12 See also Dixie Hawtin, Internet charters and principles: Trends and insights, Global Information Society Watch, 2011, 51-54, http://giswatch.org/sites/default/files/gisw_-_internet_charters_and_principles.pdf.

This study is much more than a rough comparison of the sampled documents, but it is also not as deep as being based on a discourse analysis of the underlying semantics of each document. The treatment, however, is intended to be fit for the purpose of identifying trends at a broader level.

2. Methodology

The applied methodology is an important theoretical factor for the conduct of a comparative analysis of Internet Governance statements and documents. Various approaches are available, for example (i) anifold concepts allowing indicator-driven comparisons, (ii) specific concepts based on different layer systems, and (iii) general concepts having an orientation towards substantive objectives.

2.1 Initial Background

The existing literature analyzing models for Internet Governance does not substantially support the task undertaken in this study. First attempts related to the seekingglobal action in the field of mass communication started in the early 1970s with the debates about a New World Information and Communication Order (NWICO). Thereafter, the MacBride Commission published the report "Many Voices One World" in 1980, but because of insurmountable political differences the discussions about the information and communication order then disappeared from theagenda.[13]

In the nineties of the last century, new concepts of international law wereexplored in order to overcome the sovereignty and territoriality principle leading to conflicts of jurisdiction in the global cyberspace.[14] In addition, more and more technological and political aspects have been addressed in the literature to encompass the dynamic regulatory environment. A particular focus has been laid on the development of formalized standards and networks as well as on the inclusion of informal law-making.[15]

However, an extensive doctrine by scholars providing a comparative analysis of different multilateral legal instruments, declarations, guidelines, and frameworks that relate to Internet Governance principles does not yet exist; accordingly, this study has to cover new ground. This can be seen by examining the two different kinds of literature sources available which do look at Internet Governance principles:

(1) On the one hand, there is a large number of studies generally discussing manifold aspects of Internet Governance;[16] these look at political and social topics of Internet Governance although without proceeding to a large scale comparative analysis of Internet Governance principles.

(2) On the other hand, numerous books and journal articles address specific issues which are also part of the UNESCO "Internet Universality" concept. For example, human rights, privacy, and access are debated in the context of the substantive discussions of specific issues about the legal instruments, guidelines and frameworks.[17] Nevertheless, these publications are not broadly comparative, but rather topic-centered. So far, specific

---

13   For more details see Weber, 2009, 25-28.
14   Wilske/Schiller, 1997.
15   Weber, 2014.
16   See for example Weber, 2009; Mueller, 2010; DeNardis, 2014.
17   See for example Jørgensen, 2013, to human rights and Bygrave, 2014, to privacy.

declarations, guidelines, and frameworks have rarely been reflected in connection with the assessment of ongoing developments.[18]

2.2 Concepts Based on Indicators

The development of indicators for the issues relevant in the Internet Governance context can be directed into a quantitative, a qualitative or a combined category. Quantitative factors must allow a verifiable measurement; qualitative indicators need to be reliable for further decision-making. Indicators may be disaggregated by gender, income or other characteristics. An important additional element is the accountability aspect.

Publicly available indicators mainly providing quantitative data are:

- ITU indicators[19]
- OECD indicators[20]
- CGI.Br CETIC.Br census indicators[21]

More qualitative indicators contain the following frameworks:

- *UN Special Rapporteur's Report* on the promotion and protection of the right to freedom of opinion and expression[22]
- *Ranking Digital Rights* which is still under development by a team of researchers lead by Rebecca MacKinnon, Allon Bar and Richard Danbury, and is based in New America Foundation[23]
- The *"Who has your back report"*, issued by Electronic Frontier Foundation (EFF)[24], assessing how online intermediaries respond to governments' requests for access to users' data

Quantitative and qualitative criteria are included the following documents:

- *The Web Index*, published by the World Wide Web Foundation,[25] addressing universal access, freedom and openness, relevant content and empowerment
- *Freedom on the Net Reports*, published by Freedom House,[26] analyzing the different levels of political and media freedom (obstacles to access, limits on content, violation of users' rights)

---

18 An exception might be the discussion of Recommendations and Guidelines worked out and implemented by the Council of Europe in the context of the Arab Spring movement under the heading of "Politics Through Social Networks". See Weber, 2011, 1186-1194.
19 Available at http://www.itu.int.en/ITU-D/Statistics/Pages/default.aspx.
20 Available at http://www.oecd.org/internet/broadband/oecdkeyictindicators.htm and http://www.oecd.org/sti/iecon-my/49258588.pdf.
21 Available at http://www.cetic.br/english/.
22 Available at http://http://daccess-dds-ny.un.org/doc/UNDOC/FEN/G11/132/01PDF/G1113201.pdf?OpenElement.
23 Available at http://http://rankingdigitalrights.org/project-documents/draft-criteria/.
24 Available at http://http://eff.org/who-has-your-back-2013#specific-criteria-and-changes.
25 Available at http://thewebindex.org/about/methodology/ and http://thewebindex.org./about/legacy/v2012/strucutre.
26 Available at http://freedomhouse.org/report/2013-methodology-and-checklist-question#.Uv5hKHkQ7wl.

- *Affordability Report 2013* of the Alliance for an Affordable Internet[27]

- *The World Press Freedom Indexes* published by Reporters Without Borders,[28] addressing Internet censorship and restrictions on freedom of speech

- *Corruption Perception 2013* by Transparency International[29]

- *The Global Surveillance Monitor*, a project by Privacy International[30]

- *Open Net Initiative* by Harvard University (Berkman Center) and others[31] investigating and analyzing Internet filtering

A problem with the mentioned indicators is in the discerning commonality and divergence in the main issues and objectives of the respective documents and inquiries. In addition, many indexes do not exclusively focus on Internet issues. Furthermore, most indexes produce country-specific data allowing comparisons between countries rather than between different legal frameworks and guidelines. The question could also be asked whether the collected data are sufficiently reliable.

Another problem consists in the fact that quantitative data cannot provide background and context about the appreciation of substantive principles, which leads to a solely partial perception of the Internet environment. Therefore, the mentioned indicators are not best suited to be used as methodological tool for the analysis of the available Internet Governance documents. This assessment becomes even more relevant in view of the fact that the existing Internet Governance documents are to be linked to the R.O.A.M. framework and the UNESCO objectives which is hardly possible with the mentioned indicators. As a consequence, this methodological approach is not appropriate to this study.

2.3 Concept Based on Layers

A second concept that can be applied is the so-called layer-approach in relation to Internet structure. Often, four conceptual layers are distinguished, namely

- the infrastructure and services layer (capacity and security of infrastructure as well as access and affordability as regulatory policies),

- the applications and code layer (open technologies and standards, net neutrality, security controls),

- the content layer (scope and restrictions of fundamental rights, availability of content, information sources),

- the socio-political layer (data protection, consumer rights, user capacity, surveillance).

---

27   Available at http://a4ai.org/wp-content/uploads/2014/01/Affordability-Report-2013 Final-2.pdf.
28   Available at http://rsf.org/index2014/data wpfi methodology.pdf.
29   Available at http://www.transparency.org/files/content/press and http://cpi.transperency.org/cpi2013/indetail/#myAnchor1release/2013 CPISourceDescription_EN.pdf.
30   Available at https://www.privacyinternational.org/reports/surveillance-monitor-2011-assessment-of-surveillance-across-europe.
31   Available at http://opennet.net/oni-faq.

The concept with layers has been mainly developed by Lessig[32] and Benkler[33] who were analyzing the code structure of the Internet from an engineering perspective.

If priority is given to the described layers, however, the features of the "Internet Universality" concept risk moving to the background since many elements of a technical nature do not have a major relevance for the pillars of freedom and human rights, openness, access for all, and multistakeholder participation. This assessment does not exclude that certain technical measures do have an impact on substantive rights, for example, the concept of privacy by design on the protection of personal data, or digital rights management on the scope of copyright protection.

The layer concept can nevertheless be used as a gap analysis in order to further develop new qualitative indicators for analyzing the available Internet Governance documents. The layer concept is also helping to assess the relevant gaps and to find the appropriate elements that can complement the principles' framework.

2.4 Concept Based on Substantive Objectives

Originally, the Internet has been mainly a new technology that enabled improved information and communication exchanges primarily for military purposes and research cooperation. This situation has dramatically changed: Business, security and social relationships determine the new infrastructure. The involvement of companies and individual members of civil society in the use of the Internet not only covers information and communication exchanges but also the exercise of manifold cultural activities such as the distribution of music, films, photos through different social media platforms.

The mentioned social relations entail the creation of behavioral rules and of social norms that also relate to core policies of UNESCO – such as the protection of cultural diversity, the support of knowledge societies, and the promotion of multilingualism.

The penetration of infrastructure and the number of Internet users worldwide are still substantially growing, in the future mainly in developing countries. The importance of the Internet is also mirrored by the fact that many governments around the world more closely scrutinize social media platforms and communication exchanges in civil society, since apparently the social and political implications merit attention.

The objectives in this perspective need to reflect the access and empowerment of individuals across society, economy, and politics. On the one hand, attention is needed to the ability to provide ready access to the Internet without obstacles, and the responsibility of all entities involved in the management of the Internet. On the other hand, citizens must be enabled and educated to take advantage of the new technological chances.

In addition, in order to serve as an appropriate approach for the analysis of Internet Governance documents in this study, the development of fruitful and adequate criteria around Internet objectives would need to meet the following elements:

- their facility to combine quantitative and qualitative factors where relevant;
- their facility to develop qualitative factors in a country-specific and contextualized way;

---

32   Lessig, 1999.
33   Benkler, 2006.

- their character to identify issues particularly relevant for the priorities of UNESCO and the "Internet Universality" concept.

Framed further in an approach based on substantive objectives, the Internet Universality view needs to be linked to the development of knowledge societies as a core policy of UNESCO. This factor can be understood in a broad way, including some reports which designate possible development objectives after 2015:

- The UNTT Report: Realizing the Future We Want for All;[34]
- UNDG Report: The Global Conversation Begins;[35]
- SDSN Report: An Action Agenda For Sustainable Development;[36]
- The Global Thematic Consultation on Governance;[37]
- UN Report of the High-Level Panel of Eminent Persons on the Post-2015 Development Age.[38]

Within this perspective, the subsequent analysis of the more than 50 declarations, guidelines, and frameworks as listed in the Annex to this study is done with a matrix of objectives which is based in large part on the four pillars of the R.O.A.M. framework of UNESCO ("Internet Universality" concept), namely human rights, technical/economic openness, accessibility as social dimension, and multistakeholder participation.

In addition, more particular objectives of UNESCO are addressed. Corresponding to human rights as the first pillar of the R.O.A.M. framework, it is evident that the right to freedom of expression is also a particular objective of UNESCO (information, communication, media) and that this merits special attention. In addition, there is the right to privacy (which also links to data protection), which has become a key issue of Internet Governance debates and is part of the UNESCO Internet Study, and this is discussed as separate topic.

Furthermore, two broad priorities of UNESCO, namely gender equality and the issue of sustainable development (including development issues for Africa), are assessed in separate chapters. The remaining three objectives of UNESCO, namely education (knowledge societies), science (social science, innovation) and culture (intercultural dialogue, rapprochement) are not dealt with in special chapters, but any references to these three objectives contained in the reviewed documents are summarized in a subsequent chapter after the eight main chapters.

In form of a chart, the mentioned indicators can be visualized as follows:

---

34 http://www.un.org/en/development/desa/policy/untaskteam_undf/untt_report.pdf.
35 http://www.worldwewant2015.org/the-global-conversation-begins.
36 http://unsdsn.org/files/2013/06/130613-SDSN-An-Action-Agenda-for-Sustainable-Development-FINAL.pdf
37 http://www.worldwewant2015.org/governance
38 http://www.post2015hlp.org/wp-content/uploads/2013/05/UN-Report.pdf

R.O.A.M. PRINCIPLES	EXAMPLES OF UNESCO OBJECTIVES
Freedom and Human Rights - Freedom of Expression - Privacy - Cultural Diversity and Education - Sustainable Development	**Education** (Knowledge Societies)
	Science, Social, and Human Sciences (including innovation and inclusion)
Technical / Economic Openness - Open Standards - Open Access / Architecture - Net Neutrality	**Culture** (Intercultural Dialogue, Rapprochement)
Access as Social Dimension - Universal Access - Multilingualism - Quality of Content - Ethics	**Freedom of expression** (Information, Communication, Media)
	Gender Equality
Multistakeholder Participation - Participatory Decision-making - Open Process	**Sustainable Development** (including Priority Africa)

A qualitative perspective shows that at the four pillars of the "Internet Universality" concept and the main objectives/functions of UNESCO have many linkages and relations. In principle, each pillar of the R.O.A.M. concept is at least partly mirrored in an objective of UNESCO and vice versa.

If the closest linkages are taken into account, the following summarizing statements can be made:

- The pillar on "human rights" is clearly related to the objective of freedom of expression (information, communication, media), but also to the objective of the right to education (knowledge societies). The right to cultural diversity is linked to objectives around culture (intercultural dialogue, rapprochement). Sustainable development is also embedded in a human rights environment.

- The pillar on "technical/economic openness" has a direct link to the objectives of science (social science, innovation) and sustainable development including Africa. The specific issue of net neutrality can also be mirrored in the cultural context. Covering "open access", this openness pillar is also directly related to the pillar addressing "accessibility as social dimension", i.e. the two objectives of the R.O.A.M. framework are intertwined.

- The pillar of "accessibility as social dimension" has many linkages to education (knowledge societies), science (social science, innovation), culture (intercultural dialogue, rapprochement) and freedom of expression (information, communication, media).

- The pillar on "multistakeholder participation" can be related to gender equality and sustainable development (including UNESCO's Priority Africa) as well as also to the roles of media and intermediaries within information and communication.

In a chart, the relations that will be taken up again in the context of the analysis of the reviewed documents in this study can be represented as follows:

R.O.A.M. PRINCIPLES	EXAMPLES OF UNESCO OBJECTIVES
Freedom and Human Rights	**Education** (Knowledge Societies)
Freedom of Expression	
Privacy	
Cultural Diversity and Education	**Science, Social, and Human Sciences** (including innovation and inclusion)
Sustainable Development	
Technical / Economic Openness	
Open Standards	**Culture** (Intercultural Dialogue, Rapprochement)
Open Access / Architecture	
Net Neutrality	
Accessibility (Social Dimension)	**Freedom of expression** (Information, Communication, Media)
Universal Access	
Multilingualism	
Quality of Content	
Ethics	
	Gender Equality
Multistakeholder Participation	
Participatory Decision-making	**Sustainable Development** (including Priority Africa)
Open Process	

2.5 Accountability Mechanisms in Particular

In connection with the assessment of Internet Governance principles, the importance of accountability mechanisms is an issue. These have become an important topic in the discussions about the legitimacy of international institutions as well as about Internet Governance mechanisms in particular. "Accountability" stems from the Latin word *accomptare* (to account), a prefixed form of *computare* (to calculate) used in the money lending system developed in Ancient Greece and Rome. Accountability is the acknowledgment and assumption of responsibility for policies, actions, decisions, and products within the scope of a designated role.

Accountability is a pervasive concept, encompassing political, legal, philosophical, and other aspects; each context casts a different shade on the meaning.[39] In this light, accountability can obviously be differentiated into various types, namely moral, political, administrative, managerial, economic, legal, constituency-related and professional accountability. Notwithstanding these facets, the basic elements of accountability center around the obligation of a person (the accountable) to another (the accountee), through which the former must give account of, explain and justify actions or decisions against criteria of some kind. Furthermore, the assumption of responsibility for any non-compliant behavior, fault or damage is also implied in the term accountability.

Due to the lack of a "global democracy" to which all Internet-related organizations must abide, the current global administrative bodies dealing with Internet standards are often confronted with requests to overcome accountability gaps. This issue is not only important for public oversight of these organizations' activities, but also serves the selfinterest of the respective entities. A clear definition of the authority of each body, and a justification for actions taken, contributes to their effectiveness and credibility.

Different levels can be addressed for the implementation of accountability mechanisms, namely the organizations, the projects, and the policies:[40]

- *Organization-level aspects*: Important elements here are the "democratic" structuring of the decision-making processes, giving concerned stakeholders the possibility to exercise appropriate influence on corporate governance. Typically, accountability should be bolstered through measures of institutional checks and balances.

- *Project-level aspects*: If working groups are mandated to execute certain projects, it must be ensured that through information disclosure or other safeguard policies, the concerned stakeholders can take part in the relevant developments.

- *Policy-level aspects*: Feedback mechanisms should be designed in a way that the concerned stakeholders are able to have their needs and wishes reflected in the decision-making processes. Possible means are the distribution of interactive drafts of policy provisions prior to release, or the publication of a matrix which compiles all comments, and explains how each input was addressed within the policy review, or why it was discarded.

Generally, any form of accountability is based on the assumption that objectives and standards exist against which an action or a decision may be assessed. Particularly in respect

---

39   For further details see Weber, 2009, 133.
40   For further details see Weber, 2009, 137-140.

of the policy-level, a few general requirements have been identified within recent scholarly research:[41]

- *Extended consultation of stakeholders*: New developments should be examined through consultation processes allowing potential disputes to be addressed at an early stage, and to look for solutions within due time; the design of consultation processes depends on the matters involved and on the availability of the concerned stakeholders for multistakeholder processes.

- *Improved inclusion of stakeholders*: Making activities and achieved results accountable to the stakeholders is particularly important in respect to participation of all actors. If the participatory processes are considered to be insufficient or if the concerns and comments by the stakeholders have not been adequately addressed by the competent bodies, redress measures should be available to the concerned stakeholders.

Another possibility to increase the accountability of the Internet Governance bodies consists in the implementation of some kind of intergovernmental supervision articulating closely to a multistakeholder model as reflected in the fourth pillar of the R.O.A.M. framework. As far as the form is concerned, such an approach would have to be based on a treaty-related model of governance that was agreed and implemented by a majority of countries engaged in Internet issues.

In this study, Internet Governance declarations, guidelines, and frameworks are assessed in terms of how they address or implicate accountability issues as outlined in the analysis above.

2.6 Theoretical Framework for the Analysis of the Documents

To summarize this chapter, the task has been to review possible options for an approach that could inform a theoretical analysis of Internet Governance documents.

Concepts related to Internet indicators, layers, and substantive objectives were considered. Hereinafter, a hybrid model will be applied – one that includes reference to accountability, with particular emphasis to the R.O.A.M principles of Internet Universality and the substantive objectives of UNESCO, given the purpose of this study.

A further theoretical consideration will be the issue of accountability in view of the fact that this issue impacts on the efficacy of the particular principles embodied in a particular document. Although each document has a specific context, this theoretical approach enables an analysis at a level of abstraction that is able to map presences and absences broadly, which in turn can help to inform decisions about what options UNESCO may wish to consider for its own position on Internet Governance principles.

---

41   See Weber, 2014, 79/80.

3. Analysis of Documents

3.1 General Observations of the Historical, Political, Economic, and Social Background of the Documents dealing with Internet Governance Principles

3.1.1 Overview

This study encompasses 52 declarations, guidelines, and frameworks from various international actors; the documents with all relevant details are listed in the Annex. As mentioned,[42] not all available Internet Governance documents are assessed but mainly documents having a relation to the "Internet Universality" concept of UNESCO. Out of the 52 documents the geographic origins can be summarized as follows:

- 28 documents stem from global institutions (or from several jointly acting regional institutions).
- 11 documents are based on regional initiatives.
- 13 documents have been developed by different bodies of civil society.

The originators of the documents and their form are very different. Some documents are signed by multiple actors, some by just a few actors. As far as the background is concerned, some are negotiated as consensus documents, some are to be qualified as white papers or research studies.

Prior to the detailed examination of the referenced 52 declarations, guidelines, and frameworks, all documents will be briefly described in chronological order and correspondingly be listed in the Annex. In so doing, aspects like the documents' background (historical, political, economic, social) and their legal standing (hard law, soft law) will be addressed; this approach does not mean that chronology necessarily implies progression. Without being comprehensive, the documents represent some of the most influential and representative statements as related to Internet Governance principles.

Out of the 52 documents, the quantitative analysis conducted on the basis of the above described topics being of particular relevance for UNESCO's "Internet Universality" concept shows the following results:

	Documents mentioning the aspect (out of 52)	Documents addressing the aspect in more detail (out of 52)
Access	50	22
Openness	34	17
Freedom of Expression	41	21
Privacy	36	14
Multistakeholder Part.	39	19
Ethics	19	11

---

42 See above chapter 1 (supra note 8 and 9).

	Documents mentioning the aspect (out of 52)	**Documents addressing the aspect in more detail (out of 52)**
Gender Equality	18	8
Sustainable Development	24	6
Cultural Diversity	20	8
Science	6	6
Education	24	13
Accountability	28	2

This overview provides evidence that a large number of declarations, guidelines, and frameworks have been developed and implemented during the last 25 years. They are rather disparate and mainly reflect the requirements of one (or more) specific organizations being interested to state certain principles. Positively, it can be said that the geographic origin of these documents is rather broad.

3.1.2 Short Description of the Available Internet Governance Principles

In chronological order, the following 52 declarations, guidelines, and frameworks containing Internet Governance principles have been adopted:

Ethics and the Internet

The document "Ethics and the Internet" of January 1989 is a statement of policy by the Internet Activities Board (IAB) dealing with the proper use of the Internet's resources.

SADC Declaration on Information and Communications Technology

Being in need of a coherent regional policy and strategy on information and communication technologies (ICT) that among others promotes a sustainable economic development and with regard to the fact that ICT can contribute significantly to economic development of countries, the Southern African Development Community (SADC) Member States signed the Declaration on Information and Communication Technology on 14 August 2001. The declaration recognizes the economic and social benefits of an affordable, reliable ICT infrastructure and suggests its Member States to adopt a coherent regional development policy.[43]

Manila Declaration on Accessible Information and Communication Technology

The Manila Declaration on Accessible Information and Communication Technology (ICT) is the outcome of the Interregional Seminar and Regional Demonstration Work-shop on Accessible ICT and Persons with Disabilities that took place in Manila, Philippines, on March 3 to 7, 2003. By recognizing accessibility as being an essential component of broad rights-based approaches to development (No. 2), the participants of the seminar declare among other points that accessible ICT with reasonable accommodation empowers and enables persons with disabilities to enjoy equal rights (Nos. 3, 4).

---

43   See http://www.sadc.int/documents-publications/show/830.

Recommendation on the Promotion and Use of Multilingualism and Universal Access to Cyberspace

On 15 October 2003 UNESCO's General Conference adopted a Recommendation on the Promotion and Use of Multilingualism and Universal Access to Cyberspace encompassing 25 recommendations concerning the development of multilingual content (Rec. Nos. 1-5) and public domain content (Rec. Nos. 15-22), the facilitation of access to networks and services (Rec. Nos. 6-14) and the equitable balance between the interests of rights-holders and the public interest (Rec. Nos. 23-25).

Berlin Declaration on Open Access to Knowledge in the Sciences and Humanities

With regard to the growing significance of the Internet and the importance of scientific literature being publicly available and free of charge on the Internet, the Max Planck Society, co-founder of the international Open Access movement,[44] published its Berlin Declaration on Open Access to Knowledge in the Sciences and Humanities on 22 October 2003. In view of the fact that disseminating knowledge is only half complete if the information is not made widely and readily available to the whole society (Goals of the Declaration), the Berlin Declaration defines open access contributions and supports the transition to the electronic open access paradigm.

Geneva Declaration of Principles/Geneva Plan of Action

With governments realizing the growing importance of ICT, the International Telecommunications Union (ITU) adopted a Resolution in 1998 proposing the idea of holding a World Summit on the Information Society (WSIS) under the auspices of the United Nations. In 2001, the ITU Council endorsed the approach of executing the summit in two phases, the first one in Geneva in 2003, the second one in Tunis two years later.

In the first phase, the Geneva Conference in December 2003 enacted the legally non-binding Geneva Declaration of Principles and the Geneva Plan of Action, which define the WSIS' common vision (development of inclusive information society) and a framework for measures to take for making this vision a reality.

Declaration of the Committee of Ministers on Human Rights and the Rule of Law in the Information Society

Having been drafted by the Council of Europe's Multidisciplinary Ad-hoc Committee of Experts on the Information Society and adopted by the Committee of Ministers of the Council of Europe on 13 May, 2005, the legally non-binding declaration addresses human rights like the right to freedom of expression, the right to respect for private life and the right to education on the one hand and the creation of an inclusive information society on the other hand.[45]

Tunis Agenda for the Information Society

The consensus statement of the World Summit on the Information Society, adopted on 18 November 2005 in Tunis, Tunisia, calls for the creation of an Internet Governance Forum

---

44 See http://openaccess.mpg.de/2365/en.
45 For many other Council of Europe's issue-specific declarations on the Internet, see the list at http://www.unesco.org/new/filead-min/MULTIMEDIA/HQ/CI/CI/pdf/Events/netconference_march2015_submissions/E/response_from_coe_council_of_eu- rope.pdf

and an innovative, multistakeholder governance structure of the Internet by outlining a multistakeholder concept.

International Mechanisms for Promoting Freedom of Expression

With regard to the Internet's growing relevance, the ongoing debates about Internet Governance and the outstanding importance of the right to freedom of expression, the UN Special Rapporteur on Freedom of Opinion and Expression, the OSCE Representative on Freedom of Media and the OAS Special Rapporteur on Freedom of Expression adopted the (legally non-binding) joint declaration on 21 December 2005, encompassing a number of rules for the use of the Internet.

APC Internet Rights Charter

Being of the opinion that for empowering the world's citizens within the Internet some fundamental rights need to be recognized, protected and respected, the Association for Progressive Communications (APC) published its legally non-binding APC Internet Rights Charter in November 2001 (updated in 2006).[46]

Tshwane Declaration on Information Ethics in Africa

On 7 February 2007, the participants of the African Information Ethics Conference "Ethical Challenges in the Information Age" adopted the legally non-binding Tshwane Declaration to serve as a basis for enhancing the field of information ethics in Africa.

Final Recommendations of the European Conference on "Ethics and Human Rights in the Information Society"

In order to discuss and identify the issues considered to constitute priorities for the European region and to raise the stakeholders' awareness of the ethical issues of information and communication technologies the French Commission for UNESCO in cooperation with UNESCO and the Council of Europe organized the European Conference on "Ethics and human rights in the information society" that took place from 13 to 14 September 2007 in Strasbourg. The Conference´s (legally non-binding) "Final Recommendations" complete the general report and the reports of the event's round tables, gathering and highlighting the proposals made by the participants both in their contributions and during the debates.

Maputo Declaration: Fostering Freedom of Expression, Access to Information and Empowerment of People

In the course of the UNESCO Conference on "Freedom of Expression, Access to Information and Empowerment of People" held in Maputo, Mozambique, on World Press Freedom Day (3 May 2008), the Conference's participants committed to the (legally non-binding) Maputo Declaration among others calling on UNESCO to promote freedom of expression as a universal human right and to facilitate development of general principles and best practices on access to information.

---

[46] Contemporaneously the campaign on Communication Rights in the Information Society (CRIS Campaign), established in 2001, proposedproposed to broaden the information society debates, to promote democratization of access to communica- tions and to strengthen commitments related to sustainable development (see Steve Buckley, Media freedom and the Internet: a communication rights perspective, presentation at the Conference on Guaranteeing Media Freedom on the Internet, 27 August 2004, http://www.osce.org/fom/36379?download=true.

Seoul Declaration for the Future of the Internet Economy

Having been adopted on 18 June 2008 at the conclusion of the "Ministerial Meeting on the Future of the Internet Economy", held in Seoul, Republic of Korea, the Declaration contains recommendations on how to promote the Internet economy's development through multi-stakeholder co-operation.

Madrid Privacy Declaration

The Madrid Privacy Declaration of 3 November 2009 has been published by The Public Voice, a coalition that was established in 1996 in order to promote public participation in Internet decision-making.[47] The Declaration reaffirms international instruments for privacy protection, identifies new challenges, and calls for concrete actions to achieve the goals set.

Code of Good Practice on Information, Participation and Transparency in Internet Governance

The Code of Good Practice, drafted by the Council of Europe, the United Nations Economic Commission for Europe (UNECE) and the Association for Progressive Communications (APC) of October 2010 has been developed as a legally non-binding framework of principles and guidelines helping the entities concerned with Internet Governance to maintain and improve transparency, inclusiveness and accountability as the Internet continues to grow in range, diversity and importance.[48]

Asia Declaration on Internet Governance

The declaration has been endorsed by the Centre for Policy Initiatives (CPI) on 25 June 2010 and has been signed by delegates from many Southeast Asian nations. Subsequent to the listing of observations made at the Asia-Pacific Regional Internet Governance Forum Roundtable in Hong Kong (15/16 June 2010), the declaration contains a number of recommendations to the IGF.

10 Internet Rights and Principles

The Internet Rights and Principles Dynamic Coalition (IPR), an open network of individuals and organizations dealing with the protection of human rights and active in the Internet Governance Forum online, concentrated a variety of human rights in a Charter with 21 articles and 10 principles that should form the basis of Internet Governance. The Charter as a whole was launched in March 2011 and encompasses a wide variety of substantive topics in the human rights field. Hereinafter, this study focuses on the 10 principles, although a number of the 21 articles do have relevance for further research.

Reflection and Analysis by UNESCO on the Internet

The document adopted in 2011 illustrates UNESCO's use of the Internet in the organization's fields of competence by highlighting the challenges and emerging issues arising from the fast-changing Internet environment. Besides, the document contains recommendations for the organization's future action.

---

47 See http://thepublicvoice.org/about_us/.
48 See http://www.apc.org/en/node/11199.

Joint Declaration on Freedom of Expression and the Internet

Having been adopted on 1 June 2011, the legally non-binding Joint Declaration by the United Nations (UN) Special Rapporteur on Freedom of Opinion and Expression, the OSCE Representative on Freedom of the Media, the Organization of American States (OAS) Special Rapporteur on Freedom of Expression and the African Commission on Human and Peoples' Rights (ACHPR) Special Rapporteur on Freedom of Expression and Access to Information contains general principles for promoting freedom of expression and addresses a number of Internet-related issues, namely intermediary liability, filtering and blocking, criminal and civil liability, network neutrality and access to the Internet.

African Platform on Access to Information Declaration

The (legally non-binding) African Platform on Access to Information declaration represents the outcome of the Pan African Conference on Access to Information, organized by the Windhoek+20 Campaign on Access to Information in Africa in partnership with the African Union Commission (AUC) and the Special Rapporteur on Freedom of Expression and Access to Information of the African Commission on Human and Peoples' Rights. The Conference took place in Cape Town, South Africa, September 17–19, 2011.

Declaration by the Committee of Ministers on Internet Governance Principles

Having been adopted by the Council of Europe's Committee of Ministers on 21 September 2011, the legally non-binding Declaration on Internet Governance Principles is designed to be implemented by Member States when developing national and international policies related to the Internet;[49] the policies should respect 10 principles, among others multistakeholder governance, open networks and the responsibility of states.[50]

Declaration of Internet Freedom

A group of more than 1,500 organizations, academics, startup founders and tech innovators aiming at fighting to save what they described as the free and open Internet that is central to people's freedom to communicate, share, advocate and innovate,[51] came together in 2012 in order to produce a Declaration of Internet Freedom. The legally non-binding Declaration consists of five principles, namely expression, access, openness, innovation and privacy.

Internet Governance – Council of Europe Strategy 2012-2015

On 12 March 2012, the 47 Council of Europe Member States adopted an Internet Governance strategy to protect and promote human rights, the rule of law and democracy online. The strategy to be implemented over a period of four years is setting out a coherent vision for a sustainable long-term approach to the Internet whose success will to a large extent depend on multi-stakeholder dialogue and support.

Promotion, Protection and Enjoyment of Human Rights on the Internet

On 5 July 2012, the United Nations Human Rights Council adopted a new resolution on the promotion, protection and enjoyment of human rights on the Internet that calls upon

---

49 Even though not legally binding, declarations by the Committee of Ministers possess a certain moral and political authority on the Member States. Some ideas of this Declaration have again been taken up by the Recommendation on a Guide to Human Rights for Internet Users mentioned below.
50 See http://milunesco.unaoc.org/declaration-by-the-committee-of-ministers-on-internet-governance-principles/.
51 See http://www.savetheinternet.com/internet-declaration.

all states "to promote and facilitate access to the Internet and international cooperation aimed at the development of media and information and communications facilities in all countries".

Open Standard Principles

Developed by the Institute of Electrical and Electronics Engineers (IEEE), the Internet Architecture Board (IAB), the Internet Engineering Task Force (IETF), the Internet Society and the World Wide Web Consortium (W3C), the Principles of 29 August 2012 seek to capture the effective and efficient standardization processes having made the Internet what they regard as the most important platform for innovation and borderless commerce.[52] The document consists of five fundamental principles, namely due process, broad consensus, transparency, balance, and openness. Since its launch, hundreds of proponents from industry, civil society, government and academia, as well as individual technologists and innovators have expressed their support for the principles.[53]

PEN Declaration on Digital Freedom

The non-political organization PEN International founded in 1921 connects an international community of writers and holds Special Consultative Status at the UN and Associate Status at UNESCO.[54] To summarize the organization's position on threats to free expression in the digital age, the Declaration on Digital Freedom has been approved at the PEN International Congress in Gyeongju, Republic of Korea, in 2012.

Council of Europe and Internet: Maximizing Rights, Minimizing Restrictions

In September 2012, the Council of Europe published an overview of the organization's activities with regard to the Internet.[55] The document deals with a number of rights, as for instance Internet access, freedom of expression, personal data protection, protection and empowering of children and gender equality.

UNESCO and the ethical dimensions of the information society

Emphasizing UNESCO's role in developing ethical perspectives to enable social and human progress for the information society, the document, adopted by the UNESCO's Executive Board and the General Conference on 14 September 2012, contains, among others, a number of proposals on how to address ethical dimensions of the information society.

Ethics in the Information Society: The Nine ´P´s

Aiming at becoming the leading platform for exchange and research on ethics and values, the Global Ethics Network for Applied Ethics (Globethics.net) consists of persons and institutions interested in various fields of applied ethics. The Discussion Paper *Ethics in the Information Society*: The Nine ´P´s was released on 5 May 2013, calling for value-based decisions and actions for the development of information, communication and knowledge. The so-called "Nine P's" encompass general principles, namely participation, people, profession, privacy, piracy, protection, power and policy.

---

52   See http://open-stand.org/about-us/faqs/.
53   See http://open-stand.org/about-us/.
54   See http://www.pen-international.org/who-we-are/.
55   See https://edoc.coe.int/en/internet/5990-council-of-europe-maximising-rights-minimising-restrictions.html.

Ethics Guidelines for Internet-mediated Research

The British Psychological Society's Ethics Guidelines of 2013 were prepared by the Working Party on Internet-mediated Research, convened under the aegis of the British Psychological Society's Research Board. The Guidelines outline some of the key ethics issues which researchers and research ethics committees (REC) are advised to keep in mind when considering implementing or evaluating Internet-mediated research (IMR), such as for instance confidentiality and security of online data or procedures for obtaining valid consent.

Recommendation of the Council concerning Guidelines governing the Protection of Privacy and Transborder Flows of Personal Data

Since the more extensive and innovative use of personal data in the context of the Internet is very likely to result in economic and social benefits, but will also increase privacy risks, the OECD Guidelines governing the Protection of Privacy and Transborder Flows of Personal Data of 23 September 1980 were amended on 11 July 2013.

Montevideo Statement on the Future of Internet Cooperation

Having met in Montevideo, Uruguay, for considering current issues that concern the Internet's future, the leaders of a number of organizations (some known as the "It" group) responsible for the Internet technical infrastructure's coordination[56], published their Statement on the Future of Internet Cooperation on 7 October 2013. The meeting's participants considered current issues affecting the Internet's future.

Riga Guidelines on Ethics in the Information Society

The "Riga Global Meeting of Experts on the Ethical Aspects of Information Society", held in Riga, Latvia, from 16 to 17 October 2013, concluded with the adoption of a set of legally non-binding guidelines on ethics in the information society described as reflecting the growing consensus that has emerged from the numerous fora on the ethical dimensions of the information society.[57]

Seoul Framework for and Commitment to Open and Secure Cyberspace

Being the outcome of the "Seoul Conference on Cyberspace 2013", the legally nonbinding framework, published on 18 October 2013, captures key ideas for an open and secure Internet including cybersecurity, international security, cybercrime and capacity building and calls for the United Nations to play a leading role in bringing countries together to among others develop common understandings of the use of ICT.

Final Statement: Information and Knowledge for all

From 25 to 27 February 2013, the first WSIS+10 event took place in Paris continuing the discussions of the WSIS summits in Geneva (2003) and Tunis (2005). The more than 1500 participants released a Final Statement declaring that multistakeholder processes have

---

[56] African Network Information Center (AFRINIC), American Registry for Internet Numbers (ARIN), Asian-Pacific Network Information Centre (APNIC), Internet Architecture Board (IAB), Internet Corporation for Assigned Names and Number (ICANN), Internet Engineering Task Force (IETF), Internet Society (ISOC), Latin America and Caribbean Internet Addresses Registry (LACNIC), Réseaux IP Européens Network Coordination Centre (RIPE NCC), World Wide Web Consortium (W3W).

[57] See http://www.unesco.org/new/en/media-services/single-view/news/riga_ethics_expert_meeting_outcomes_now_available/back/9597/#.VHM8uXeB_e4.

become an essential and unique approach to engagement in addressing issues affecting the knowledge and information societies, highlighted the importance to protect and promote freedom of expression, as well as promoting universal access to information and knowledge as part of the free flow of information. The statement was endorsed by UNESCO Member States at their General Conference in 2014.

OECD Principles of Internet Policy Making

After the adoption of the OECD Recommendation on Internet Policy Making Principles in 2011 that were endorsed by all 34 OECD Member countries, together with Colombia, Costa Rica, Egypt and Lithuania, the organization, following its mission of promoting policies that will improve the economic and social well-being of all people around the world, published its (final) Principles of Internet Policy Making in 2014.

Joint Declaration on Universality and the Right to Freedom of Expression

The Joint Declaration by the UN Special Rapporteur on Freedom of Opinion and Expression, the OSCE Representative on Freedom of the Media, the OAS Special Rapporteur on Freedom of Expression and the ACHPR Special Rapporteur on Freedom of Expression and Access to Information was presented at the UNESCO World Press Freedom Day event in Paris, France, on 6 May 2014. The Declaration contains a number of recommendations for States and other actors to protect and defend the right to freedom of expression including on the Internet.

Communication on Internet Policy and Governance

Proposing a basis for a common European vision for Internet Governance the legally non-binding Communication issued by the European Commission on 12 February 2014 addresses the main policy areas relevant to the whole Internet Governance ecosystem (pp. 2/3). The document, among other points, focuses on Internet Governance principles' development, on core Internet functions and on the strengthening of the existing multistakeholder model.

Delhi Declaration for a Just and Equitable Internet

On February 14 to 15, 2014, a global meeting ("Towards a Just and Equitable Internet") of civil society actors was held in Delhi aiming at formulating a progressive response to issues of global governance of the Internet. [58] This meeting's key outcome was the formation of the Just Net Coalition and the drafting of the legally non-binding Delhi Declaration.

Recommendation on a Guide to Human Rights for Internet Users

As further developed from the above mentioned Declaration of 2011, the Council of Europe's Guide to Human Rights for Internet Users of 16 April 2014 aims at protecting and supporting human rights and fundamental freedoms on the Internet in all Council of Europe Member States. In so doing, the Recommendation serves as a tool for Internet users to learn about the online existing human rights, their possible limitations, and available remedies for such limitations (Introduction).

NETmundial Multistakeholder Statement

The NETmundial Multistakeholder Statement is the non-binding outcome of the Global Multistakeholder Meeting on the Future of Internet Governance, "a bottom-up, open, and

---

58   See http://www.southsolidarity.org/towards-a-just-and-equitable-internet/.

participatory process involving thousands of people from governments, private sector, civil society, technical community, and academia from around the world" (Preamble), that took place on 23 and 24 April 2014 in Sao Paulo, Brazil.

Paris Declaration

Having been released at the UNESCO World Press Freedom Day International Conference in Paris, France, on 5 to 6 May 2014, the Declaration contains a number of recommendations made by media and human rights experts concerning the right to access to information and the development and follow-up of an independent media landscape on all platforms. The demands contained in the Paris Declaration were later forwarded to the Open Working Group of the United Nations as an input for the post-2015 Sustainable Development Goals (SDG).

EU Human Rights Guidelines on Freedom of Expression Online and Offline

In adopting guidelines concerning freedom of expression both online and offline during its Foreign Affairs meeting held in Brussels, on 12 May 2014, the Council of the European Union said that it reaffirms the crucial role of freedom of expression and freedom of opinion within a democratic society.

Towards a Collaborative, Decentralized Internet Governance Ecosystem

By highlighting key elements of Internet Governance, the report by the Panel on Global Internet Cooperation and Governance Mechanisms, published in May 2014, supports the further development of a collaborative Internet Governance ecosystem. The Panel recognizes, fully supports, and adopts the IG Principles produced in the NETmundial Statement as the basis of Internet Governance (p. 2).[59]

African Union Convention on Cyber Security and Personal Data Protection

On 28 June 2014, heads of States of the African Union (AU), a group of 54 African governments launched in 2002, approved the legally non-binding African Union Convention on Cyber Security and Personal Data Protection.

Lyon Declaration on Access to Information and Development

The legally non-binding Lyon Declaration of 18 August 2014, launched at the World Library and Information Congress (IFLA), held in Lyon, France, from 16 to 22 August 2014, aims at positively influencing the United Nations post-2015 development agenda including dimensions relevant to online information.[60]

African Declaration on Internet Rights and Freedoms

On 28 August 2014, the Pan African initiative to promote human rights standards and principles of openness in Internet policy issued an *African Declaration on Internet Rights and Freedoms*. Being built on well-established African human rights documents including the African Charter on Human and Peoples' Rights of 1981, the *Windhoek Declaration on Promoting an Independent and Pluralistic African Press* of 1991, the *African Charter on Broadcasting* of 2001, the *Declaration of Principles on Freedom of Expression in Africa* of 2002, and the *African Platform on Access to Information Declaration* of 2011, the African Declaration

---

59 Therefore, this report will not be discussed in detail within each category.
60 See http://conference.ifla.org/past-wlic/2014/ifla80/node/522.html.

on Internet Rights and Freedoms is intended to elaborate on the principles which are necessary to uphold human and people's rights on the Internet, and to cultivate an Internet environment that meets Africa's social and economic development needs and goals best.

Bali Road Map

The Roles of the Media in Realizing the Future We Want For All On 28 August 2014, the participants of the three-day meeting on "The Role of Media in Realizing the Future We Want For All", organized by Indonesia and UNESCO,[61] adopted the Bali Road Map "to realize the potentials of the media to contribute to sustainable development, and to promote the inclusion of a goal acknowledging the importance of freedom of expression and independent media in the post-2015 Sustainable Development Goals". This document includes interrelated aspects.

Nairobi Declaration on the Post 2015 Development Agenda

On 13 November 2014, African media as well as civil society stakeholders and media experts from other parts of the world met in Nairobi, Kenya, at the Global Forum for Media Development's (GFMD) African Regional Workshop on the Post-2015 Development Agenda. Concluding the workshop, the 33 participants adopted the Nairobi Declaration on the Post 2015 Development Agenda comprising a number of observations and recommendations. First of all, that a sustainable development depends on the participation of informed people in governance processes and decision-making, which in turn require access to information and the effective exercise of the right to freedom of expression, including the existence of free and independent media. The Declaration, among other points, refers to the importance of including the goal to ensure good governance and effective institutions within the United Nations Sustainable Development Goals to be developed.

Right to Privacy in the Digital Age

The Resolution adopted by the United Nations General Assembly on 19 November 2014 recalls and slightly extends the United Nations Resolution 68/167 of 18 December 2013[62] and emphasizes the importance of protecting people's rights to privacy both offline and online, and expresses reservations with regard to the impact that surveillance and interception of communications may have on human rights.

3.1.3 Conclusion

The short description of the more than 50 documents, touching on some of their historical, political, economic, and social background, shows their manifold origins and scopes. Often, depending on the given situation, only a limited number of principles is enshrined in the documents, namely those principles having a special importance in a given context. In addition, the wording for similar principles is often not identical since their formulation is context-driven.

As far as the legal quality is concerned, most documents have mainly a moral or reputational "force". This assessment is particularly appropriate in respect of documents, which have been developed during conferences or similar events. If the originator of a document is an

---

61   UNESCO In collaboration with the Ministry of Communication and Information Technologies of the Republic Indonesia, the Indonesian National Commission for UNESCO, the Indonesian Press Council and the United Nations Information Centre.

62   See http://www.un.org/ga/search/view_doc.asp?symbol=A/RES/68/167.

established and esteemed international organization (for example UNESCO, OECD, or the Council of Europe), the soft law character of the declarations/recommendations does not lead to binding obligations yet the institutional framework increases the indirect incentive for Member States to comply with the respective principles.

On this basis, hereinafter all documents will be assessed on whether and to what extent they deal with those objectives of UNESCO policies which have been defined as central in Chapter 2, namely access and openness, freedom of expression, privacy, ethics, participation, gender equality, sustainable development, and culture/science/education.

Thereby, it should be noted that the right to freedom of expression includes the right to seek and receive as well as impart information. The first part of the right (seek and receive) is largely covered under "access", and the "impart" dimensions is the subsection on freedom of expression, although the two dimensions are interrelated. On the Internet, limits of access are not only a fetter on seeking and receiving information, but also on imparting. As an example, the blocking of a social networking site in one domain prevents not only the consumption of its contents, but also the possibility of contributing to the respective content (such as by way of comments or postings).

3.2 Access and Openness

As mentioned in Chapter 2, the "Internet Universality" highlights the principle of "technical/economic openness" (incl. open access) and the principle of "accessibility as social dimension". Since access and openness are interrelated (as also elaborated by the 10 Internet Rights and Principles and their underlying Charter), the two issues are presented together hereinafter.

3.2.1 Access

3.2.1.1 Contents of Documents

Almost all (50 out of 52) of the reviewed documents make reference to the necessity of granting all interested users access to the Internet and the information and knowledge contained therein.

Several of these documents address access to the Internet; this is the case for the following documents:

The Internet Activities Board's paper on *Ethics and the Internet*, the *SADC Declaration on Information and Communications Technology (ICT)*, the WSIS *Tunis Agenda for the Information Society*, the *International Mechanisms for Promoting Freedom of Expression*, the *Tshwane Declaration on Information Ethics in Africa*, the *Madrid Privacy Declaration*, the *Code of Good Practice on Information, Participation and Transparency in Internet Governance*, the *Asia Declaration on Internet Governance*, the *10 Internet Rights and Principles*, the Human Rights Council's document on the *Promotion, protection and enjoyment of human rights on the Internet*, the *Declaration by the Committee of Ministers on Internet Governance Principles*, the *Free Press' Declaration of Internet Freedom*, the *Open Standard Principles*, the *PEN Declaration on Digital Freedom*, the *Council of Europe and Internet: Maximizing Rights, Minimizing Restrictions*, the UNESCO Discussion Paper on *Ethics in the Information Society: The Nine 'P´s*, the *Ethics Guidelines for Internet-mediated Research*, the *Recommendation of the Council concerning Guidelines governing the Protection of Privacy and Transborder Flows of Personal Data*, the *Montevideo Statement on the Future of Internet Cooperation*, the *Riga*

Guidelines on Ethics in the Information Society, the *Seoul Framework for and Commitment to Open and Secure Cyberspace*, the OECD *Principles for Internet Policy Making*, the *Joint Declaration on Universality and the Right to Freedom of Expression*, the UNESCO-linked *Paris Declaration*, the European *Commission's Communication on Internet Policy and Governance*, the *Delhi Declaration for a Just and Equitable Internet*, the Report by the Panel on Global Internet Cooperation and Governance Mechanisms *Towards a Collaborative, Decentralized Internet Governance Ecosystem*, and the United Nations Resolution on the *Right to Privacy in the Digital Age*.

A small number of documents explicitly deals with access to information and knowledge, namely the UNESCO *Recommendation on the Promotion and Use of Multilingualism and Universal Access to Cyberspace*, the *Manila Declaration on Accessible Information and Communications Technology*,[63] the Max Planck Society's *Berlin Declaration on Open Access to Knowledge in the Sciences and Humanities*, the UNESCO-linked *Maputo Declaration* dealing with freedom of expression, access to information and the empowerment of people, the *African Platform on Access to Information Declaration*, the *NETmundial Multistakeholder Statement*[64] and the *Lyon Declaration on Access to Information and Development*.[65]

The following documents address access to information and knowledge in more detail:

Geneva Declaration of Principles/Geneva Plan of Action (WSIS)

Highlighting the importance of getting access to information, ideas and knowledge the Declaration aims at empowering all, especially the poor living in remote, rural and marginalized urban areas, to achieve equitable and affordable access to information and ICT (Nos. 1, 14, 19, 21-28). In addition, the Plan of Action contains a number of suggestions on how to grant all interested access to the Internet for contributing to an inclusive Information Society (No. 10.a-j).

Declaration of the Committee of Ministers on Human Rights and the Rule of Law in the Information Society (CoE)

Stating that limited or no access to ICT can deprive individuals of the ability to fully exercise their human rights, the Declaration emphasizes the importance of encouraging access to ICT and their use by all without discrimination (I.3) and requests Member States to allow citizens the widest possible access to content (I.1) by promoting education to allow all those interested, in particular children, to acquire the necessary skills to work with the ICT and to assess the information's quality (I.3).

APC Internet Rights Charter

The Charter's first and third topic address Internet access for all and access to knowledge in great detail by discussing the impact of access on development and social justice (No. 1.1), the right to access to infrastructure irrespective of where persons live (No. 1.2), the right to obtain skills (No. 1.3), the right to interface, content and applications accessible to all (No. 1.4), the right to equal access for men and women (No. 1.5), the right to affordable access (No. 1.6), the right to access to a workplace (No. 1.7), the right to public access (No. 1.8), the right to access through creation of content that is culturally and linguistically

---

63 Outcome of the Interregional Seminar and Regional Demonstration Workshop on Accessible ICT and Persons with Disabilities, Manila, Philippines, March 3-7, 2003.
64 Outcome of the Global Multistakeholder Meeting on the Future of Internet Governance.
65 Released by the International Federation of Library Associations and Institutions.

diverse (No. 1.9), the right to access to knowledge (No. 3.1) and the right to access to publicly-funded information (No. 3.3).

Final Recommendations of the European Conference on "Ethics and Human Rights in the Information Society"

The Final Recommendations address the development and implementation of a policy of universal Internet access that should be inspired by ethical values of solidarity and social justice (No. 14).

Seoul Declaration for the Future of the Internet Economy (OECD)

With regard to access, the Declaration's signatories, among others, declare to facilitate the convergence of digital networks, etc. through policies that uphold the open, decentralized and dynamic nature of the Internet (p. 6) policies should also encourage a more efficient use of the radio frequency spectrum (p. 6), foster creativity in the development, use and application of the Internet through policies that make public sector information widely accessible in digital format (p. 7), and ensure that the Internet economy is truly global through policies that support access to the Internet expanded access (p. 8).

Reflection and Analysis by UNESCO on the Internet (UNESCO)

Rating access to information and knowledge as being a prerequisite for building inclusive knowledge societies, the document points to the fact that most up-to-date knowledge is still only accessible to those who can afford access, at the disadvantage of those in developing and least developed countries (Nos. 22, 23). However, the document comes to the conclusion that "barriers of access to the Internet will diminish, bringing to the fore questions relating to the use of the Internet in all regions of the world" (No. 41).

Joint Declaration on Freedom of Expression and the Internet (Special Rapporteurs of UN, OSCE, OAS and ACHPR)

The Declaration refers to the States' duty to promote universal access to the Internet being necessary to promote respect for other rights as for instance the rights to education, to health care, to work and to free elections (Nos. 6.a, 6.e, 6.f) and contains a number of obligations States should fulfil (Nos. 6.e, 6.f).

Internet Governance – Council of Europe Strategy 2012-2015

The Council of Europe's Strategy discusses access in a variety of scopes, for instance with regard to the protection of the Internet's universality, integrity, and openness (No. 8) and in the context of maximizing and minimizing rights and freedoms for Internet users (No. 9), and maximizing the Internet's potential to promote democracy and cultural diversity (No. 13).

Recommendation on a Guide to Human Rights for Internet Users (CoE)

The Recommendation contains a number of suggestions on how to improve access to information, namely by providing Internet users affordable and non-discriminatory access (Access and non-discrimination, No. 1.2), by obligating public authorities to make reasonable efforts and to take specific measures in order to facilitate access for people living in rural and geographical remote areas, being on low income or having special needs (Access and non-discrimination, No. 1.3), by making information about the relevant law policies accessible

(Privacy and data protection, No. 4) and by granting people online access to education and cultural content (Education and literacy, Nos. 1, 2).

Final Statement: Information and Knowledge for all (WSIS+10)

The Final Statement rates broadband related infrastructure and access to the Internet as being one of the key aspects in achieving the information and knowledge societies and emphasizes that still two thirds of the world's population lack access (p. 3).The Statement, among other issues, invites all stakeholders to further promote universal access to information, to facilitate the open access to scientific information and to make efforts addressing the challenges in the availability, affordability and quality of access (pp. 3, 4).

EU Human Rights Guidelines on Freedom of Expression Online and Offline (Council of the European Union)

Aiming at ensuring and protecting non-discriminatory access to information for all individuals, both online and offline, the Guidelines refer to the European Union's ambition to support the efforts of third countries to increase and improve the citizens' Internet access (No. 33.b) and to promote unhindered, uncensored, and non-discriminatory access to ICT and online services (No. 33.c). As to that, it is important to guarantee that access to the Internet will not be subject to unjustified restrictions (Annex I, p. 16).

African Union Convention on Cyber Security and Personal Data Protection

Dealing with cybersecurity and the protection of personal data, the Convention addresses the access to personal data in more detail. As for instance, in order to guarantee a functioning e-commerce, the Convention obligates States to ensure that any person exercising e-commerce activities shall provide to those for whom the goods and services are meant, easy, direct and uninterrupted access using non-proprietary standards (p. 8). According to the Convention's right to access, any natural person whose personal data are to be processed may request from the controller a range of information (p. 23).

African Declaration on Internet Rights and Freedoms (Pan African Initiative)

To realize its development potential, the Internet needs to be accessible, available and affordable for all persons in Africa (Preamble; Right to Information, Principle No. 4); cutting off or slowing down Internet access can never be justified (Internet Access and Affordability, Principle No. 2). This makes it necessary to adopt policies and regulations fostering non-discriminatory access to the Internet, to facilitate high-speed Internet access and to develop as well as to share best practices about how to improve Internet access for all sectors of the society (points about Access and Affordability). Data and information held by government should be made publically accessible (remarks to Right to Information and Open Data).

Bali Road Map (Global Media Forum)

The Road Map proposes that governments work towards granting universal access to the Internet in a manner that ensures equal access and participation for men and women (Governments, No. 5).

Nairobi Declaration on the Post 2015 Development Agenda (Global Forum for Media Development)

Rating access to information and independent media as being critical for democratic and economic development (Observations), the Declaration recommends that the United Nations Sustainable Development Goals shall include the right of people to achieving access to free and independent media.

3.2.1.2 Conclusion

Almost all reviewed documents discuss the access to information and knowledge, showing the right's importance. While many of the documents treat the right only superficially, some (about 45 percent) contain more detailed remarks and concrete improvement suggestions.

Documents not addressing access to information and knowledge are the *Recommendation of the Council concerning Guidelines governing the Protection of Privacy and Transborder Flows of Personal Data* and the *Montevideo Statement on the Future of Internet Cooperation*. In these cases, it can be assumed that the lack of reference is due to the document's specific direction.

3.2.2 Openness

3.2.2.1 Contents of Documents

A total of 34 of the 52 reviewed documents deals with the Internet's (technical) openness.

Some of the documents address the topic of openness without mentioning further aspects; this is the case for the following documents:

The UN *Manila Declaration on Accessible Information and Communications Technology*, the WSIS *Tunis Agenda for the Information Society*, the *Final Recommendations of the European Conference on "Ethics and Human Rights in the Information Society"*, the *Maputo Declaration*, the *Code of Good Practice on Information, Participation and Transparency in Internet Governance*,[66] the *Reflection and Analysis by UNESCO on the Internet*, the *African Platform on Access to Information Declaration*, the *Internet Governance – Council of Europe Strategy 2012-2015*, the Human Rights Council's document on *The promotion, protection and enjoyment of human rights on the Internet*, the *Open Standard Principles*, the *Council of Europe and Internet: Maximizing Rights, Minimizing Restrictions*, the *Recommendation of the Council concerning Guidelines governing the Protection of Privacy and Transborder Flows of Personal Data*, the *Delhi Declaration for a Just and Equitable Internet*, the *EU Human Rights Guidelines on Freedom of Expression Online and Offline*, the *Panel Report Towards a Collaborative, Decentralized Internet Governance Ecosystem*, the *Lyon Declaration on Access to Information and Development*, and the UN document *The Right to Privacy in the Digital Age*.

Two documents explicitly deal with openness, namely the *Berlin Declaration on Open Access to Knowledge in the Sciences and Humanities (Max Planck Society)* and the *Seoul Framework for and Commitment to Open and Secure Cyberspace (Conference Outcome)*.

The following documents address openness in more detail:

---

66 Released by the CoE, the UNECE and the APC.

Recommendation on the Promotion and Use of Multilingualism and Universal Access to Cyberspace (UNESCO)

The document recommends regional organizations and forums to encourage the establishment of inter and intra-regional networks within a global network in an open competitive environment, and invites Member States and international organizations to promote open access solutions (Rec. Nos. 12, 18).

Geneva Declaration of Principles/Geneva Plan of Action (WSIS)

According to the Geneva Declaration of Principles, access to information and knowledge can be promoted by increasing awareness among all stakeholders of the possibilities offered by different software models, including open-source and free software (No. 27). Besides this, the Declaration strives to promote open access initiatives for scientific publishing and calls for the use of open, interoperable demand-driven standards (Nos. 28, 44).

The Geneva Plan of Action, among others, calls for encouraging initiatives to facilitate access, including free and affordable access to open access journals and open archives for scientific information (No. 10), asks governments to promote the development and use of open standards and open source software (Nos. 13, 23), and promotes open access initiatives to make scientific information affordable and accessible in all countries on an equitable basis (No. 22).

APC Internet Rights Charter

The Charter supports the rights to share information with open and free participation in knowledge flows, to free and open source software and to open technological standards (Nos. 4.1, 4.2, 4.3). It also calls for the openness of all decision-making processes related to Internet Governance and the Internet's development (6.2), the right to open architecture (No. 6.4) and the right to open standards (No. 6.5).

Seoul Declaration for the Future of the Internet Economy (OECD)

For promoting the Internet Economy's development, the Declaration's signatories declare to uphold the open nature of the Internet (p. 6) and to maintain an open environment that supports the free flow of information (p. 7).

Asia Declaration on Internet Governance (Centre for Policy Initiatives)

According to the Declaration, open access to information is the right of every individual and is fundamental to knowledge and capacity-building (Key Observations, No. 1). Rating openness as a key to a democratic and open society, the Asia Declaration states that intimidation and state censorship facilitate self-censorship which in turn undermines democracy and openness (Key Observations, No. 1).

10 Internet Rights and Principles (Internet Rights and Principles Coalition)

The document's third and eighth principle address the importance of openness by stating that everyone shall have open access to web-content, free from any discrimination, filtering or traffic control. According to the tenth principle, the governance of the Internet shall be based on openness. As mentioned, further details are addressed in the underlying Charter.

Declaration by the Committee of Ministers on Internet Governance Principles (CoE)

According to the Committee of Ministers' eighth Internet Governance principle, the open standards of the Internet should be preserved. Addressing open networks, the ninth Internet Governance principle states, among others, that all Internet users should have the greatest possible access to Internet-based content and services, whether or not they are offered free of charge.

Declaration of Internet Freedom (Free Press)

The Declaration's main objective is to support a free and open Internet. The document's third principle addresses openness and calls for keeping the Internet an open network.

Ethics in the Information Society: The Nine ´P´s (British Sociological Society)

Addressing the importance of getting open Internet access for free or for affordable costs, the Discussion Paper calls upon governments to include support for open access repositories and asks public and private actors to develop open access and open publishing initiatives (pp. 10, 11). In addition, the WSIS should support privacy in coherence with open access to information (p. 16).

Final Statement: Information and Knowledge for all (WSIS+10)

The participants of the first WSIS+10 review event invite all stakeholders to recognize the importance of maintaining an open Internet based on open standards development processes (p. 3), to facilitate the open access to scientific information in all regions of the world, especially in the least developed countries, (p. 4) and to support research and facilitate frameworks to favour open access to information and knowledge while respecting intellectual property rights (p. 4).

OECD Principles of Internet Policy Making

The document addresses the promotion of an open, distributed and interconnected nature of the Internet, stating that the Internet's openness to new devices and services has played an important role in its success, and refers to globally accepted, consensus-driven technical standards that also supported the Internet's openness (p. 21). For ensuring this openness, technology neutrality and appropriate quality for all Internet devices need to be maintained (p. 21).

Communication on Internet Policy and Governance (European Commission)

Stating that an open and free Internet facilitates the social and democratic progress worldwide (Introduction) and that the Internet should remain an open and free, unfragmented network of networks (p. 11), the European Commission declares to engage with stakeholders to clearly define the role of public authorities consistent with an open and free Internet (p. 5). In addition, it is also important to support the involvement of the European Internet industry in the development of open internet standards (p. 9).

NETmundial Multistakeholder Statement (Conference Outcome)

Arguing in favour of an open and distributed Internet architecture, the Statement calls for upholding the end-to-end nature of the Internet (p. 5). Besides that, the governance of the Internet should be open and should promote open standards (pp. 6, 7). In the context of the Points to be further discussed beyond NETmundial, the Statement addresses the importance of continuing the discussion of the Open Internet (p. 11).

African Declaration on Internet Rights and Freedoms (Pan African Initiative)

The Declaration's first Key Principle deals with openness, stating that the Internet should have an open and distributed architecture and should be developed based on open pluralistic standards; additionally, the protection of social and economic openness is addressed. Since open data can empower people to take a more active part in public affairs, the Declaration calls on the technical communities to actively respect and promote the open standards of the Internet. In addition, the Declaration states that the Internet Governance framework must, among others, be open (Key Principle No. 12).

3.2.2.2 Conclusion

About two third of the reviewed documents discuss or even thoroughly address the Internet's (technical) openness, half of it with more detailed remarks and concrete improvement suggestions.

Documents not addressing the term openness are the Internet Activities Board's document on *Ethics and the Internet*, the *SADC Declaration on Information and Communications Technology*, the *Declaration of the Committee of Ministers on Human Rights and the Rule of Law in the Information Society*, the *International Mechanism for Promoting Freedom of Expression*, the *Tshwane Declaration on Information Ethics in Africa*, the *Madrid Privacy Declaration*, the Joint *Declaration on Freedom of Expression and the Internet*, the *PEN Declaration on Digital Freedom, the UNESCO and the ethical dimensions of the information society*, the *Ethics Guidelines for Internet-mediated Research*, the *Montevideo Statement on the Future of Internet Cooperation*, the *Riga Guidelines on Ethics in the Information Society*, the *Recommendation on a Guide to Human Rights for Internet Users*, the *Joint Declaration on Universality and the Right to Freedom of Expression*, the *Paris Declaration*, the *African Union Convention on Cyber Security and Personal Data Protection*, the *Bali Road Map and the Nairobi Declaration on the Post 2015 Development Agenda*.

Based on these 18 cases, corresponding to about one third of the reviewed documents, the assumption seems to be justified that the lack of reference is due to the document's specific direction (mainly ethics, privacy and freedom of expression).

3.3 Freedom of Expression

Although not all documents focus on the importance of ensuring freedom of expression in the Internet, their majority (41 out of 52) tackles the issue.

3.3.1 Contents of Documents

Recommendation on the Promotion and Use of Multilingualism and Universal Access to Cyberspace (UNESCO)

The UNESCO Recommendation states that both the definition and the adoption of best practices and guidelines should be encouraged among information producers, users and service providers with due respect to freedom of expression (Rec. No. 22).

Geneva Declaration of Principles/Geneva Plan of Action

The Declaration refers to the fact that everyone has the right to freedom of expression (No. 4). The Plan of Action highlights the media's essential role regarding the preservation of the right to freedom of expression and recommends media to take appropriate measures, consistent with the right to freedom of expression, for combating illegal and harmful content in media activities (No. 24).

Declaration of the Committee of Ministers on Human Rights and the Rule of Law in the Information Society (CoE)

Addressing freedom of expression in detail, the Declaration refers to ICT's opportunities for all to enjoy freedom of expression and to the right's challenges, namely state and private censorship (I.1); it contains a number of suggestions for improvements.

Tunis Agenda for the Information Society (WSIS)

Without addressing the aspect in more detail, the Tunis Agenda refers to the fact that measures undertaken to ensure Internet stability and to fight cybercrime must protect and respect freedom of expression as contained in the relevant parts of the Geneva Declaration of Principles (No. 42).

International Mechanism for Promoting Freedom of Expression (Special Rapporteurs of UN, OSCE, OAS and ACHPR)

Corresponding to the document's name, the Declaration contains a number of mechanisms on how to promote freedom of expression online.

APC Internet Rights Charter

The Charter's second theme deals with the right to freedom of expression and association and, in that regard, emphasizes the importance of protecting the right to freedom of expression by both, governments and non-state actors (No. 2.1). With respect to the Internet's main function of being a medium for the exchange of (private and public) views, it is necessary to ensure that individuals may freely express their opinions and ideas when using the Internet (No. 2.1). Indications relevant to freedom of expressions can also be found within the context of the Charter's right to the Internet as an integrated whole (No. 6.7) and to recourse in the case of infringements (No. 7.2).

Final Recommendations of the European Conference on "Ethics and Human Rights in the Information Society"

According to the Final Recommendations, the right to freedom of expression should be reaffirmed and promoted (No. 11). With regard to the fact that a user's capacity for autonomy works as an important condition for ensuring his or her freedom of expression online, attention should be paid to the significance of strange traffic data, to technical filtering measures and to the blocking of information by public authorities; furthermore, private actors working as gatekeepers to public communication spaces (Internet access providers, search engine providers) merit attention.

Maputo Declaration (UNESCO Conference)

Aiming at fostering the fundamental right to freedom of expression as being essential to democratic discourse, the Declaration invites Member States to foster freedom of expression by implementing commitments to grant the law's exercise and by preventing measures that hinder freedom of expression online. It calls on media to raise the Internet users' awareness about the right to freedom of expression. In conclusion, the Declaration requests UNESCO to sensitize governments, legislators and public institutions in respect of the importance of the right to freedom of expression.

Seoul Declaration for the Future of the Internet Economy (OECD)
The Declaration does not directly consider the right to freedom of expression but points out that the Internet economy's further expansion will also support the freedom of expression (p. 4).

Madrid Privacy Declaration (Public Voice Coalition)
Without explicitly dealing with the right to freedom of expression, the Declaration contains a warning that the failure to protect privacy puts other freedoms at risk, including the right to freedom of expression.

Asia Declaration on Internet Governance (Centre for Policy Initiatives)
Assessing restrictions of the right to freedom of expression as one of the threats to open societies (Key Observation No. 1), the Asia Declaration's signatories recommend to immediately address the increasing number of laws suppressing and restricting the right to freedom of expression especially within developing countries (Recommendation No. 1).

10 Internet Rights and Principles (Internet Rights and Principles Dynamic Coalition)
Dealing with expression and association, the document's fifth principle grants every Internet user the right to freely seek, receive, and impart information online; as mentioned, further details are addressed in the wider underlying Charter.

Reflection and Analysis by UNESCO on the Internet
Stating that freedom of expression belongs to the "heart of UNESCO's mandate", the analysis (No. 27) points to the increasing challenge for governments to respond to illegal Internet content without affecting freedom of expression (No. 29). UNESCO's response to that predicament should be the promotion of a legal environment ensuring freedom of expression.

Joint Declaration on Freedom of Expression and the Internet (Special Rapporteurs of UN, OSCE, OAS and ACHPR)
As the name suggests, the Joint Declaration exclusively deals with the right to freedom of expression and acceptable limitations and restrictions.

African Platform on Access to Information Declaration (Conference Outcome)
The Declaration rates the right to freedom of expression as being a fundamental right (Preamble) and highlights the last 20 years' significant progress in protecting this right.

Declaration by the Committee of Ministers on Internet Governance Principles (CoE)
Following the Committee of Ministers' Declaration, traffic management measures having an impact on the right to freedom of expression must meet the requirements of international

law on the protection of freedom of expression and access to information (Internet Governance Principle No. 9).

Declaration of Internet Freedom (Free Press)
The Declaration's first basic principle deals with expression and the prohibition of censorship in the Internet.

Internet Governance – Council of Europe Strategy 2012-2015
This Strategy describes freedom of expression as being of utmost importance (No. 3), especially with regard to the fact that people spend more and more time online. The document focuses on raising awareness for the right's protection (Nos. 10 and 13.h), and in this context also on the creation of a balance between guaranteeing the fundamental right to freedom of expression and protecting other individuals' reputation as protected under the European Convention on Human Rights (No. 9.c).

Promotion, protection and enjoyment of human rights on the Internet (Human Rights Council)
By addressing the importance of considering human rights and in particular the right to freedom of expression on the Internet, the Human Rights Council refers to the fact that the same rights that people have offline must also be protected online (No. 1) Accordingly, the Council decides to continue its consideration of the promotion, protection and enjoyment of the right to freedom of expression and other human rights (No. 5).

PEN Declaration on Digital Freedom
The PEN Declaration grants all individuals the right to express themselves freely through digital media without fearing any reprisal or persecution by governments (Principle No. 1). In addition, governments are committed to actively protect the right to freedom of expression by enacting and enforcing effective laws and standards (Principle No. 1). The Declaration is also intended to apply to the private sector, and technology companies in particular (Principle No. 4).

Council of Europe and Internet: Maximizing Rights, Minimizing Restrictions
Referring to the increasing number of search engines, social networks, etc. that dramatically changed the media landscape by allowing individuals to actively participate in the Internet, the Council of Europe's information paper refers to the right to freedom of expression enshrined in Art. 10 European Convention on Human Rights and the right's challenges due to the blocking, filtering and censoring of Internet content. In that regard, the document points to the Council of Europe's activities for promoting freedom of expression, as for instance the above described Internet Governance principles of 2011 *(Declaration by the Committee of Ministers on Internet Governance Principles)*.

Ethics in the Information Society: The Nine ´P´s (Global Ethics Network for Applied Ethics)
Rating freedom of expression as being a fundamental value for the knowledge society (p. 9), the Discussion Paper requests governments and the society as a whole to respect the right's exercise while avoiding moral harm and violation of persons' integrity (pp. 13, 15).

Recommendation of the Council concerning Guidelines governing the Protection of Privacy and Transborder Flows of Personal Data

Without discussing the issue in detail, the Recommendation recognizes that the Guidelines' principles should not be interpreted in a manner unduly limiting the right to freedom of expression (p. 14).

Riga Guidelines on Ethics in the Information Society (Conference Outcome)

Affirming freedom of expression as being a fundamental right, the Guidelines recognize that the same principles of freedom of expression apply equally to the Internet and other uses of ICT, as they apply to traditional forms of media (Guideline No. 1). The Guidelines call for promoting dialogue between all stakeholders so as to ensure legal protection and respect of the right to freedom of expression (Guideline No. 6) and recommend the sharing and promotion of best practices regarding the right to freedom of expression (Guideline No. 7).

Seoul Framework for and Commitment to Open and Secure Cyberspace (Conference Outcome)

The Framework does not deal with the right to freedom of expression in more detail, but highlights the importance of protecting the same rights offline and online, in particular the right to freedom of expression (p. 1).

Final Statement: Information and Knowledge for all (WSIS+10)

Emphasizing the importance of protecting and promoting the right to freedom of expression (p. 2), the participants of the WSIS+10 event invite all stakeholders to respect this right (p. 3).

Joint Declaration on Universality and the Right to Freedom of Expression (Special Rapporteurs of UN, OSCE, OAS and ACHPR)

The Joint Declaration addresses the right's fundamental role, and expresses concerns about infringements as well as the frequent attempts to justify these activities. To guarantee the right's exercise, the Declaration contains a number of recommendations for States and other actors.

Communication on Internet Policy and Governance (European Commission)

For supporting freedom of expression, the Commission declares to improve its development assistance programs (p. 8).

Delhi Declaration for a Just and Equitable Internet (Conference Outcome)

The Internet is a space for free expression (Principle No. 1), granting all users this right (Principle No. 15).

Recommendation on a Guide to Human Rights for Internet Users (CoE)

Addressing the right to freedom of expression, the Guide gives a detailed explanation on the meaning of seeking, receiving and imparting information without interference and regardless of frontiers.

NETmundial Multistakeholder Statement (Conference Outcome)

The Statement's first mentioned Internet Governance principle deals with the freedom of expression by repeating the wording of Art. 19 of the *Universal Declaration of Human Rights*[67] (Internet Governance Principles). The NETmundial's participants identified a number of issues needing further discussion in appropriate fora, among them the question of net neutrality and how to enable freedom of expression in this context (Roadmap IV.)

Paris Declaration (UNESCO)

Stating that the right to freedom of expression encompassing press freedom and the right to access information helps to promote human development and a culture of peace (p. 1), and can be seen as an enabler of many goals relevant to the post-2015 development agenda (p. 2), the Declaration calls on the relevant intergovernmental organizations to support "the inclusion of a specific goal to ensure good governance and effective institutions along with relevant indicators relating to freedom of expression" (p. 3). Journalists, Internet intermediaries etc. are invited to participate in the ongoing debates about the right to freedom of expression (p. 3).

EU Human Rights Guidelines on Freedom of Expression Online and Offline (Council of the European Union)

Dealing with freedom of expression online and offline, the Guidelines contain a number of challenges that the right is facing but provide practical guidance on how to contribute to preventing potential violations of freedom of expression.

Towards a Collaborative, Decentralized Internet Governance Ecosystem (Panel Report)

The Report does not directly address freedom of expression but refers to the NETmundial Multistakeholder Statement and the remarks regarding freedom of expression contained therein.

African Union Convention on Cyber Security and Personal Data Protection

Related to the promotion of cybersecurity, the Convention refers to the States' duty to consider freedom of expression while adopting legal measures for combating cyber-crime (p. 27).

Lyon Declaration on Access to Information and Development (Conference Outcome)

The Declaration does not discuss freedom of expression in detail but states that the Internet's sustainable development must take place in a human-rights based framework promoting, protecting and respecting freedom of expression as being central to an individual's independence (Declaration No. 2.d).

African Declaration on Internet Rights and Freedoms (Pan African Initiative)

Rating freedom of expression as being essential for the Internet's development, the Declaration's third Key Principle addresses freedom of expression by slightly changing the wording of Art. 19 of the *Universal Declaration of Human Rights*. The Declaration, unlike most of the other documents described, analyzes the right's scope and contains a number of suggestions on how to safeguard the right's exercise.

---

67 See http://www.un.org/en/documents/udhr/.

Bali Road Map (Global Media Forum)

The Road Map asks governments to respect the right to freedom of expression as being a fundamental right and an enabler of the post-2015 development agenda goals (Governments, No. 1). Governments are also invited to work towards realising the right's exercise by promoting the inclusion of a goal recognizing the right's importance (Governments, Nos. 5, 15). UNESCO and the international community shall promote greater understanding about the importance of the right to freedom of expression and shall ensure that aid programmes take into account the importance of having an efficient right to freedom of expression (UNESCO and the international community, Nos. 1, 2, 8).

Nairobi Declaration on the Post 2015 Development Agenda (Global Forum for Media Development)

The Declaration's recommendations state that the United Nations Sustainable Development Goals replacing the Millennium Development Goals should respect the right to freedom of expression.

The Right to Privacy in the Digital Age

Without addressing freedom of expression in detail, the United Nations Resolution indicates the interaction between the right to privacy and freedom of expressions (p. 2), and points out that unlawful or arbitrary surveillance may lead to a violation of the right to freedom of expression (p. 3).

3.3.2 Conclusion

Summarizing the large number of relevant documents, it can be said that the right to freedom of expression plays an important role within the reviewed declarations, guidelines, and frameworks of Internet Governance principles. While most of the documents treat the right rather vaguely, some discuss the challenges that freedom of expression is facing and provide practical guidance on how to contribute to preventing potential violations of the right. A general assessment is that the declarations point to a need for increased coherence in the application of the right to freedom of expression online.

3.4 Privacy

In total 36 of the examined 52 documents (70 percent) deal with privacy issues in the Internet.

3.4.1 Contents of Documents

Ethics and the Internet (Internet Activities Board)

The document does not explicitly address privacy issues. However, the Internet Activities Board characterizes any human behavior which purposely destroys the privacy of users as being unethical and unacceptable (p. 2).

Recommendation on the Promotion and Use of Multilingualism and Universal Access to Cyberspace (UNESCO)

Without addressing the aspect in detail, the UNESCO Recommendation invites Member States to consider privacy within the context of the right of universal online access to public and government-held records (Rec. No. 15).

Geneva Declaration of Principles/Geneva Plan of Action

The Declaration postulates the strengthening of privacy by ensuring the protection of data and privacy as being a prerequisite for the information society's development (No. 35). Privacy issues are also addressed within the context of the ethical dimensions of the Information Society (No. 56) by stating that the use of ICT and content creation should respect human rights and fundamental freedoms of others, including personal privacy. According to the Plan of Action, all actors in the Information Society should protect privacy and personal data (No. 25.c). For building confidence and security in the use of ICT, the document recommends that governments and other stakeholders actively promote user education and awareness about online privacy and the means of protecting privacy (Nos.12.c, 13.i), and seeks to strengthen the trust and security framework with initiatives or guidelines (among others) dealing with privacy rights and data protection (No. 12.f). Privacy aspects should also be considered in the context of e-health (Nos. 18.a, 18.d).

Declaration of the Committee of Ministers on Human Rights and the Rule of Law in the Information Society (CoE)

Even though ICT measures such as Privacy Enhancing Technologies (PET) can be used to protect privacy and any use of ICT should respect the right to private life and private correspondence, such technical advances also involve the risk of posing serious threats to these rights (I.2.). Accordingly, the Declaration requests Member States to promote frameworks for selfand co-regulation by private sector actors aiming at protecting the right to respect for private life and private correspondence (I.2.) and invites private sector actors to initiate and develop selfand co-regulatory measures (II.3).

Tunis Agenda for the Information Society (WSIS)

According to the Tunis Agenda, measures undertaken to ensure Internet stability as well as to fight cybercrime and to counter spam must also protect and respect Internet users' privacy (No. 42). Additionally, all stakeholders are invited to ensure respect for privacy and the protection of personal information and data (No. 46).

APC Internet Rights Charter

Theme 5 of the Charter considers the issues of privacy, surveillance and encryption and emphasizes that communication on the Internet should be entitled to use tools which encode messages to ensure private communication (No. 5.3). Besides, the right to the Internet as an integrated whole should not be fragmented by an invasion of privacy (No. 6.7).

Seoul Declaration for the Future of the Internet Economy (OECD)

By sharing the vision that the Internet Economy will improve the quality of all citizens' lives by among others enabling new forms of civic engagement and participation that promote privacy (pp. 4/5), the Seoul Declaration proposes to strengthen confidence and security, through policies that ensure the protection of digital identities, personal data as well as the privacy of individuals online (p. 8). For ensuring the Internet Economy's globality, policies that increase cross-border co-operation of governments and enforcement authorities in the areas of improving cyber-security as well as protecting privacy shall be established (p. 9). In conclusion, the declaration invites the OECD to assess the existing OECD instruments addressing privacy (p. 10).

Madrid Privacy Declaration (Public Voice Coalition)

Considering privacy as being a fundamental human right set out in a wide range of human rights instruments and national constitutions, the Declaration's initiators (civil society) reaffirm their support for Privacy Enhancing Technologies (No. 3), urge countries to establish comprehensive frameworks for privacy protection (No. 5) and monitor existing legal frameworks for privacy protection (No. 6). In addition, the Declaration recommends detailed research into the adequacy of new techniques for determining whether in practice such methods safeguard privacy (No. 8), and it calls for the establishment of a new international framework for privacy protection (No. 10).

Asia Declaration on Internet Governance (Centre for Policy Initiatives)

The Declaration discusses privacy in the context of cybersecurity. According to the Declaration, a definition of the term cybersecurity must include elements addressing the right to privacy; besides, privacy rights should not be sacrificed in the name of security (Key Observation No. 1).

10 Internet Rights and Principles (Internet Rights and Principles Dynamic Coalition)

The document's fifth principle deals with privacy and data protection by stating that everyone shall have the right to privacy in the Internet including freedom from surveillance, the right to use encryption and the right to operate anonymously. As mentioned, further details are addressed in the underlying Charter.

Reflection and Analysis by UNESCO on the Internet

The UNESCO document emphasizes the Internet's challenges in particular as regards privacy and security (Nos. 2, 24, 30).

African Platform on Access to Information Declaration (Conference Outcome)

The Declaration deals with privacy in the context of health issues (Application of Principles No. 8). Even though governments have a duty to provide access to information including access to health care services, the Declaration states that the enhanced access to health-related information shall not preclude the right to privacy (Application of Principles No. 8).

Declaration by the Committee of Ministers on Internet Governance Principles (CoE)

Without explicitly mentioning privacy issues, the Declaration refers to the fact that traffic management measures which have an impact on the right to respect for private life must meet the requirements of international law concerning the right to respect for private life (Internet Governance Principle No. 9).

Declaration of Internet Freedom (Free Press)

The Declaration's fifth basic principle calls for privacy protection and the defense of everyone's ability to control how their data and devices are used.

Internet Governance – Council of Europe Strategy 2012-2015

Trust in the Internet is closely connected with the protection of personal data and respect for privacy on the Internet (p. 1, Executive Summary); accordingly, the strategy's goals encompass the improvement of the Internet users' data protection and privacy (No. 5). In order to achieve these objectives, the strategy's lines of action state that efforts to protect privacy should become more and more important (No. 10). Since users' privacy must be a central concern and priority for democracies (No. 10.1), the strategy recommends (among others) the renewal of the Convention for the Protection of Individuals with regard to Automatic Processing of Personal Data (No. 10.1a.). Besides, the right to privacy of citizens in the new media environment should be secured by promoting the development of privacy securing measures and tools for children and their families (No. 10.1f.).

PEN Declaration on Digital Freedom

The Declaration states that full freedom of expression entails a right to privacy, too, and that all existing international laws and standards apply to digital media (Principle No. 3.d), and it requests governments to meet international laws and standards of privacy (Principle No. 3.e).

Council of Europe and Internet: Maximizing Rights, Minimizing Restrictions

By dealing with the question of how to protect personal data and privacy online since the Internet encompasses both opportunities and risks for privacy, the Council of Europe refers to its activities regarding the modernization of its *Convention for the Protection of Individuals with regard to Automatic Processing of Personal Data* of 1981.[68] In addition, the organization asks its Members States to work with operators for safeguarding human rights by, among others, empowering Internet users to protect their own privacy, and by increasing the transparency of the functioning of search engines.

Ethics in the Information Society: The Nine ´P´s (Global Ethics Network for Applied Ethics)

Since threats to privacy are constantly arising, a reasonable balance is needed between privacy and security needs (p. 16). As to this, the working paper requests governments to enact and enforce reasonable privacy safeguards for their citizens, invites companies to ensure greater attention to the ethical dimension of business by paying more attention to the individuals' privacy, and asks Internet intermediaries to be more transparent about governmental requests concerning data access (p. 17, Recommendations). Privacy issues are also addressed in the context of the protection of children and young people by inviting Internet and social networking providers to ensure comprehensible and accessible privacy mechanisms (p. 21).

Ethics Guidelines for Internet-mediated Research (Working Party on Internetmediated Research)

The document refers to the four principles outlined in the Code of Human Research Ethics of 2011 (p. 6).[69] In the context of the first principle dealing with respect for the Internet users' autonomy and dignity online privacy is also discussed (p. 6), by among others referring to the fact that privacy issues are very problematic and need additional careful considerations.

---

68 See http://conventions.coe.int/Treaty/en/Treaties/html/108.htm.
69 See http://www.bps.org.uk/sites/default/files/documents/code_of_human_research_ethics.pdf.

Recommendation of the Council concerning Guidelines governing the Protection of Privacy and Transborder Flows of Personal Data (OECD)

Recognizing that member countries have a common interest in promoting and protecting privacy, that more extensive uses of personal data increase privacy risks, and that the continuous flows of personal data across global networks strengthen the need for improved interoperability among privacy frameworks (p. 11), the Council recommends member countries to demonstrate leadership and commitment to privacy protection (p. 12).

Riga Guidelines on Ethics in the Information Society (Conference Outcome)

The Guidelines do not explicitly deal with privacy issues. Nevertheless, for upholding the ethical dimensions of the Information Society, the document advocates the promotion of discussions between all stakeholders as to ensure legal protection and respect of human rights in social media, especially the rights for freedom of expression and privacy (Guideline No. 6), for sharing and promoting best practices on the respect of privacy protection (Guideline No. 7), and for protecting online privacy (Guideline No. 14).

Seoul Framework for and Commitment to Open and Secure Cyberspace (Conference Outcome)

Without explicitly dealing with privacy issues, the Framework refers to the fact that the successful fight against the criminal misuse of ICT requires the development of privacy protection mechanisms, too (p. 5).

Final Statement: Information and Knowledge for all (WSIS+10)

The Final Statement invites all stakeholders to protect privacy (p. 3).

OECD Principles for Internet Policy Making

With regard to the fact that a strong privacy protection is needed for enabling the Internet to fulfil its social and economic potential, the OECD Principles for Internet Policy Making want privacy rules to be based on globally recognized principles as for instance, the OECD Guidelines Governing the Protection of Privacy and Transborder Flows of Personal Data (p. 11, No. 9). For strengthening consistency and effectiveness in privacy protection at a global level, privacy rules should also consider other fundamental rights of members of a given society (p. 11, No. 9).

Communication on Internet Policy and Governance (European Commission)

The European Commission's Communication refers to the technical community's role regarding the protection of the Internet users' privacy (p. 10) and the technical community's efforts in establishing approaches to specification setting based on public policy concerns (p. 8).

Delhi Declaration for a Just and Equitable Internet (Conference Outcome)

The Declaration's 16th principle grants everyone the right to privacy by using the Internet without mass surveillance.

Recommendation on a Guide to Human Rights for Internet Users (CoE)

Stating that everyone (regardless of the age) has the right to private and family life in the Internet which includes the protection of personal data and respect for the confidentiality of correspondence and communications (Privacy and data protection, children and young people), the Recommendation contains information for Internet users regarding the risks of the Internet and how to protect privacy online. By way of example, the Recommendation refers to the public authorities' and private companies' obligations in handling private data, the prohibition of general surveillance or interception measures, and the protection of privacy in the workplace (Privacy and data protection, Nos. 2,4,5). Children and young people are entitled to special protection when using the Internet, as for instance by receiving information in a language appropriate for their age and by getting special protection from interference with their physical, mental and moral welfare (Children and young people, Nos. 2, 5).

NETmundial Multistakeholder Statement (Conference Outcome)

For protecting the right to privacy, the document's first Internet Governance Principle (Human Rights and Shared Values) calls for reviewing procedures, practices and legislation concerning (among others) the surveillance of communications, their interception and the collection of personal data.

EU Human Rights Guidelines on Freedom of Expression Online and Offline (Council of the European Union)

The EU Human Rights Guidelines aim at protecting all rights both, offline and online, including among others the right to privacy (No. 6).

Towards a Collaborative, Decentralized Internet Governance Ecosystem (Panel Report)

With regard to its goal of outlining a framework for an Internet Governance ecosystem that fits the velocity and the transnational nature of the Internet, the Report encourages initiatives for how the global community can work together to establish minimum baselines for privacy and security (Recommended Next Steps No. 6, p. 26). By adopting the principles produced in the *NETmundial Multistakeholder Statement* the Panel is also adopting the statement's first Internet Governance Principle referring to privacy.

African Union Convention on Cyber Security and Personal Data Protection

The Convention considers the protection of personal data and private life as being a major challenge for both governments and other stakeholders which requires a balance between the use of ICTs and the protection of the citizens' privacy (p. 2). In so doing, a number of articles with regard to personal data protection contain remarks regarding privacy, in particular Art. 8 (Objective of this Convention with respect to personal data), Art. 10 (Preliminary personal data processing formalities), Art. 14 (Specific principles for the processing of sensitive data), and Art. 25 (Legal measures).

Lyon Declaration on Access to Information and Development (Conference Outcome)

Sustainable development requires a human rights-based framework promoting, protecting and respecting privacy as being central to each individual's independence (Declaration No. 2.d). Hence, in the context of access to information and data, the Declaration requests the United Nation's Member States to respect the right to individual privacy (Declaration No. 6.a).

African Declaration on Internet Rights and Freedoms (Pan African Initiative)

Based on the underlying IRPC Charter, the Declaration's eighth Key Principle refers to privacy on the Internet stating that everyone has the right to privacy online, to communicate anonymously on the Internet and to use appropriate technology to ensure secure, private and anonymous communication. Except for restrictions provided by law, there should not be any other limitations in exercising the right to privacy. For realizing online privacy, the Declaration suggests a transparent privacy policy allowing Internet users to gain knowledge about data collected, to correct inaccurate information, to protect unauthorized data from disclosure (Personal Data Protection), and to prohibit mass or indiscriminate surveillance by law (Surveillance). Next to the call on all African stakeholders, including regional and sub-regional bodies, national governments, civil society organizations, media institutions and the relevant technology and Internet companies to endorse the *African Declaration on Internet Rights and Freedoms*, the authors invite the UNESCO to integrate the Declaration into its "Priority Africa" strategies and to develop model laws protecting online privacy. In addition, companies operating in Africa are invited to translate their policies on privacy and data protection into local languages and to make them easily accessible on their respective country-level websites.

Bali Road Map (Global Media Forum)

Without addressing privacy in detail, the Road Map invites Governments to protect privacy while collecting information which is related to development issues and making the information accessible to the public (Governments, No. 8).

The Right to Privacy in the Digital Age

In order to ensure privacy protection, both offline and online, the United Nations Resolution calls upon all States to respect and protect the right to privacy in the Internet (4.[a]), to take measures enabling to avoid privacy violations (4.[b]), to review their existing procedures, practices, and legislations regarding the surveillance of communications (4.[c]), to establish and foster independent oversight mechanisms (4.[d]) and to provide individuals whose right to privacy has been violated by unlawful or arbitrary surveillance with access to an effective remedy (4.[e]).

3.4.2 Conclusion

Summarizing, it can be said that privacy issues play an important role within the reviewed declarations, guidelines, and frameworks of Internet Governance principles. Over the years, the intensity and the concretization of the privacy documents has increased and the geographic scope is enlarged. Recent revelations about governmental surveillance and the growing exposure to data protection violations explain this trend.

3.5 Ethics

3.5.1 Contents of Documents

Only about one third (19) of the examined declarations, guidelines, or frameworks refer to the necessity of implementing basic ethical rules in connection with the use of the Internet.

Ethics and the Internet (Internet Activities Board)

The document deals with ethics in general and gives examples for unethical behavior. In so doing, the Internet Activities Board characterizes as unethical and unacceptable any activity which purposely seeks to gain unauthorized access to the resources of the Internet, disrupts the intended use of the Internet, destroys the integrity of computerbased information and/or compromises the privacy of users (p. 2).

Recommendation on the Promotion and Use of Multilingualism and Universal Access to Cyberspace (UNESCO)

According to the UNESCO Recommendation, ICT training should not be limited to the provision of technical competences but should also include awareness of ethical principles and values (Rec. No. 19).

Geneva Declaration of Principles/Geneva Plan of Action

Seeking to ensure that everyone can benefit from the ICT opportunities, the Geneva Declaration of Principles addresses the ethical dimension of the Information Society as being a key principle (No. 19) and states that the Information Society should respect peace and uphold fundamental values like freedom, solidarity and shared responsibilities (No. 56). By acknowledging the importance of ethics for the Information Society, the Declaration invites all actors to take appropriate actions and preventive measures (No. 59). In that context, the document calls for the responsible use and treatment of information by the media in accordance with the highest ethical standards (No. 55).

The *Geneva Plan of Action* advocates that the Information Society should be subject to universally held values, should promote the common good and should prevent abusive uses of ICT (No. 25). It invites all stakeholders to increase their awareness of the Internet usage's ethical dimensions (No. 25.c), and further encourages all relevant stakeholders to continue research on ethical dimensions of ICT (No. 25.d).

Tunis Agenda for the Information Society (WSIS)

The Tunis Agenda calls for the responsible use and treatment of information by the media in accordance with the highest ethical and professional standards (No. 90).

Tshwane Declaration on Information Ethics in Africa (Conference Outcome) Understanding ethics in the Internet as being the field of critical reflection on moral values and practices with regard to the production, storage, distribution and access to knowledge (Preamble), and noting the necessity of ethical reflections on norms and values (Preamble), the Declaration points to the fact that information ethics should play an important role in African education and policy for fostering social, cultural and economic development (Preamble). In so doing, one of the Declaration's principles says that policies and practices regarding the generation, dissemination and utilisation of information in and about Africa should be grounded on ethics based on universal human values, human rights and social justice.

Final Recommendations of the European Conference on "Ethics and Human Rights in the Information Society"

Highlighting the main proposals made by the participants in their contributions and during the debates, the Final Recommendations call for proclaiming universal ethical principles (No. 2), for taking action to monitor issues relating to ethics in knowledge societies (No. 3), for translating principles into codes of ethics at all levels (No. 4), and for encouraging and developing ethics (No. 6).

Seoul Declaration for the Future of the Internet Economy (OECD)

Without explicitly dealing with ethics, the Declaration aims at promoting the secure and responsible use of the Internet respecting international social and ethical norms.

Reflection and Analysis by UNESCO on the Internet

UNESCO considers the adoption of ethical standards for the Internet as being essential for sustainable development (Nos. 16, 34, 35). By addressing ethical aspects of Internet use (pp. 2/3), UNESCO suggests ethics training for science journalists (No. 11) and supports relationships among ethicists, social scientists, policy-makers and civil society for assisting Member States enacting effective policies (No. 13).

African Platform on Access to Information Declaration (Conference Outcome)

The Declaration calls on media to respect professional ethics and journalism standards without addressing the issue in more detail (p. 8).

UNESCO and the ethical dimensions of the information society

This document addresses UNESCO's key role in developing ethical perspectives to enable social and human progress for the information society (p. 7), the organization's contribution to the international debate on the ethical dimensions of the information society (p. 8), the ongoing global efforts in the field of ethical dimensions of the information society (p. 8), and proposals for possible ways that UNESCO could address ethical dimensions of the information society (pp. 9, 10).

Ethics in the Information Society: The Nine ´P´s (Global Ethic Network for Applied Ethics)

In line with the title, the Discussion Paper deals with ethical issues related to the Internet. Calling for value-based decisions and actions for the development of information, communication and knowledge (Preface), the document among others discusses ethical values (p. 8), ethics of information professions (p. 14) and ethics of regulation and freedom (p. 24). Following this, the discussion paper advocates for an ethical dimension as a fundamental pillar of the Information Society post-2015 (p. 26). It requests that the principles of an ethical information society should be elaborated by experts under the aegis of the international organizations concerned and that enterprises in the private sector also take initiatives for the introduction of ethics into the Information Society (p. 27). The future governance of the Internet should be based upon ethical values (pp. 27/28).

Ethics Guidelines for Internet-mediated Research (Working Party on Internetmediated Research)

Aiming at outlining some key issues which researchers are advised to keep in mind when considering implementing or evaluating an Internet-mediated research study, the document considers the main ethics principles as outlined in the British Psychological Society's Code of Human Research Ethics of 2010,[70] namely respect for the autonomy and dignity of persons, scientific value, social responsibility as well as maximizing benefits and minimizing harm (p. 2).

Riga Guidelines on Ethics in the Information Society (Conference Outcome)

By highlighting the relevance of ethical principles to all stakeholders, the participants of the *Riga Global Meeting of Experts on the Ethical Aspects of Information Society* agreed upon a number of guidelines for upholding the Information Society's ethical dimension. In so doing, they aim at encouraging debates on the ethical challenges of the information society (Guideline No. 2), propose to raise awareness about the ethical implications of the ICT use and development (Guideline No. 4), and demand the support of the participation of all interested stakeholders in the discussion of information ethics (Guideline No. 5). By highlighting that policy-makers should be sensitized to give consideration to ethical principles (Guideline No. 8), the Guidelines further aim at supporting capacity building of policy-makers for the ethically informed development of frameworks and decision tools, based on universal human rights and ethical principles (Guideline No. 10).

Final Statement: Information and Knowledge for all (WSIS+10)

The document invites all stakeholders to discuss the ethical challenges of emerging technologies and the information society (p. 3).

Joint Declaration on Universality and the Right to Freedom of Expression (Special Rapporteurs of UN, OSCE, OAS and ACHPR)

Without discussing ethical aspects in detail, the Declaration's signatories recommend media to play a positive role in countering discrimination, stereotypes, prejudices and biases by adhering to the highest professional and ethical standards (2.c.).

EU Human Rights Guidelines on Freedom of Expression Online and Offline (Council of the European Union)

As with the *Joint Declaration on Universality and the Right to Freedom of Expression*, the *EU Human Rights Guidelines on Freedom of Expression Online and Offline* do not directly dwell on ethical aspects. Pointing to the fact that an open society based on the rule of law needs an independent and pluralistic media environment offline and online for operating effectively, the Guidelines state that the EU will encourage the promotion of mechanisms such as media ethic codes within third countries to enhance press accountability (No. 32.g).

Bali Road Map (Global Media Forum)

Without addressing ethics in detail, the Road Map supports the promotion of respect for the highest professional and ethical standards in journalism (Media outlets, media professionals and social media users, No. 1).

---

70 See http://www.bps.org.uk/sites/default/files/documents/code_of_human_research_ethics.pdf.

Nairobi Declaration on the Post 2015 Development Agenda (Global Forum for Media Development)

The Declaration refers to the poor ethical values in some sectors of society, including governments, the private sector and the general public (Observations), and recommends media regulatory bodies, media professional associations and unions, as well as the media community in general to ensure that the media in different countries maintain ethical standards (Recommendations).

3.5.2 Conclusion

In contrast to the importance of granting people access to information and knowledge, freedom of expression or privacy in regard to the Internet, to date, ethical aspects in the World Wide Web have gained less attention. But even though only a relatively small fraction of the reviewed documents concerns ethical aspects in the Internet, the majority of those are fairly detailed. In addition, ethics has been increasingly addressed during the last few years all over the world in a range of statements which can be interpreted as sign for its growing importance.

3.6 Multistakeholder Participation

3.6.1 Contents of Documents

As in case of the previously discussed freedom of expression, about 70 percent of the documents reviewed (39 out of 52) address the issue of participation in the Internet matters. In some cases, the treatment is rather general, in others, implementation aspects are mentioned. The multistakeholder element, addressing participation in different ways and using different terms, mainly appears in the most recent documents, for example in connection with the NETmundial Conference (Sao Paolo, April 2014).

SADC Declaration on Information and Communications Technology

The Declaration does not explicitly mention the term multistakeholder participation but refers to community participation in general (p. 3). In so doing, the Declaration's signatories undertake to enable all people regardless of their gender, financial background, or geographical origin to participate in the information society on an equal footing.

Manila Declaration on Accessible Information and Communication Technology

Online participation for everyone depends on the access to both the physical environment and information in general (No. 2). For empowering and enabling persons with disabilities to full, effective, and equal participation in social, economic, cultural life, as well as in the exercise of civil and political rights, the seminar and workshop have focused on accessible ICT with reasonable accommodation (No. 3).

Recommendation on the Promotion and Use of Multilingualism and Universal Access to Cyberspace (UNESCO)

Without addressing multistakeholderism in detail, the Recommendation points to the fact that the development of new ICT is also presenting challenges for ensuring the participation of all in the global information society (Preamble).

Geneva Declaration of Principles/Geneva Plan of Action

According to the *Geneva Declaration of Principles* the Internet's management, encompassing both technical and public policy issues, should involve all stakeholders and relevant intergovernmental and international organizations (No. 49). In addition, the Declaration emphasizes the importance of empowering women to become key actors in the Information Society (No. 12) and refers to the significance of partnerships, in particular between developed and developing countries, for the promotion of global participation (No. 33). In order to stimulate the participation of all stakeholders, the Declaration suggests developing local content suited to domestic or regional needs (No. 53).

Stating that the effective participation of and cooperation among all stakeholders is indispensable for the Information Society's development (No. 8) the *Geneva Plan of Action* calls for the establishment of a working group on Internet Governance (No. 13) to, among others, develop a common understanding of the respective roles and responsibilities of the governments, existing intergovernmental and international organizations, private sector and civil society (No. 13.b)iii). In addition, the Plan of Action encourages governments to develop ICT policies fostering innovation and entrepreneurship with particular reference to the promotion of participation by women (No. 13.l).

Declaration of the Committee of Ministers on Human Rights and the Rule of Law in the Information Society (CoE)

Within the reviewed documents, the first mention of the term "multistakeholder" can be seen in the *Declaration of the Committee of Ministers on Human Rights and the Rule of Law in the Information Society*. In so doing, the heading "A multi-stakeholder governance approach for building the Information Society" is followed by a summary of the different stakeholders' roles and responsibilities (II.). Besides that, with regard to the right of having free elections, the Declaration invites Member States to examine the use of ICT in fostering democratic processes for strengthening the citizens' participation (I.7).

Tunis Agenda for the Information Society (WSIS)

The Tunis Agenda refers to the importance of enhancing and ensuring the participation of developing countries and all stakeholders, especially girls and women, in Internet Governance mechanisms and the emerging new society (Nos. 18, 31, 51-53, 65, 90, 91). The Agenda states that there is "a need to initiate, and reinforce, as appropriate, a transparent, democratic, and multilateral process, with the participation of governments, private sector, civil society and international organizations, in their respective roles" (No. 61); it also "acknowledges that multi-stakeholder participation is essential to the successful building of a people-centred, inclusive and development-oriented Information Society and that governments could play an important role in this process" (No. 97).

APC Internet Rights Charter

Public participation can be intensified by providing affordable, fast, and easy access to the Internet (No. 1.1). In the context of granting equal rights to access for men and women, the Charter also calls for enabling women to fully participate in all areas related to Internet development (No. 1.5).

Tshwane Declaration on Information Ethics in Africa (Conference Outcome)

The Declaration does not deal with the participation of all stakeholders as mentioned above but with the greater participation of African scholars in the field of information ethics within the international scholarly community.

Final Recommendations of the European Conference on "Ethics and Human Rights in the Information Society"

Without explicitly mentioning multistakeholder participation, the Final Recommendations ask for translating ethical principles into codes of ethics at all levels with the participation of all interested actors, i.e. producers or providers of information systems, servers, search engines, electronic media and discussion forums (No. 4). Moreover, the creation of a vast amount of public domain information can be seen as a precondition for the democratic participation of all in public life (No. 15).

Maputo Declaration (UNESCO Conference Outcome)

By emphasizing the importance of having media diversity (public service, commercial, community), the Declaration points to the community broadcasters' contribution in fostering underrepresented or marginalized populations and especially women's access to information and participation in decision-making processes. The Declaration also highlights the inclusion of information and media literacy in school curricula for enhancing all citizens' participation in public debate.

Seoul Declaration for the Future of the Internet Economy (OECD)

The Seoul Declaration does not deal with multistakeholder participation but shares the vision that the Internet economy will strengthen the capacity to improve the quality of all citizens' life by enabling new forms of civic engagement and participation (p. 5).

Madrid Privacy Declaration (Public Voice Coalition)

Without mentioning the term multistakeholder participation, the Madrid Privacy Declaration calls for the establishment of a new international framework for privacy protection accomplished with the full participation of civil society (No. 10).

Code of Good Practice on Information, Participation and Transparency in Internet Governance (CoE, UNECE, APC)

Rating multistakeholder participation as one of the main principles for the Internet's development and governance (Introduction), the Code addresses the issue in more detail. In so doing, the document states that the participation from all stakeholders has become a generally accepted norm for Internet Governance that needs to be preserved (Principle No. 1) since the Internet's development is closely linked to the engagement of all types of Internet participants (Principles Nos. 2, 3).

Asia Declaration on Internet Governance (Centre for Policy Initiatives)

The Declaration applauds the work of the first Asia-Pacific Regional Internet Governance Forum towards building multistakeholder discussions on Internet Governance (p. 1), but does not deal with the issue in more detail. However, the Declaration addresses the importance of ensuring active remote participation in the IGF meetings (Recommendation No. 7).

10 Internet Rights and Principles (Internet Rights and Principles Dynamic Coalition)

Stating that the governance of the Internet should be based on human rights and social justice, the document recommends that this shall happen in a transparent and multilateral manner based on inclusive participation (No. 10).

Reflection and Analysis by UNESCO on the Internet

One of UNESCO's goals is to strengthen public participation in policy and decisionmaking (No. 27).

Joint Declaration on Freedom of Expression and the Internet (Special Rapporteurs of UN, OSCE, OAS and ACHPR)

The Joint Declaration mentions the Internet's power to promote public participation and notes the mechanisms of the IGF's multistakeholder approach (p. 1).

African Platform on Access to Information Declaration (Conference Outcome)

The Conference's participants call on the governments of Member States of the African Union to join and implement multistakeholder efforts and invite private companies to join multistakeholder initiatives (pp. 8/9). In that regard, governments are invited to ensure that the existing legal frameworks allow all stakeholders (individuals, civil society organizations, media organizations and private businesses) to fully enjoy access to the Internet for fostering their active participation in socio-economic life (Application of Principles No. 1). The Declaration refers to the governments', civil society's and media's obligation to facilitate women's equal access to information for enabling them to participate in public life (Application of Principles No. 4).

Declaration by the Committee of Ministers on Internet Governance Principles (CoE)

According to the Committee of Ministers' Declaration, the development and implementation of Internet Governance arrangements should ensure the full participation of all stakeholders including governments, the private sector, civil society, the technical community and individual Internet users by taking into account their specific roles and responsibilities (Nos. 2, 4). The development of international policies related to the Internet as well as Internet Governance arrangements should also enable full and equal participation of all stakeholders from all countries (No. 2).

Internet Governance – Council of Europe Strategy 2012-2015

Emphasizing that the Council of Europe fully supports the multistakeholder model of Internet Governance for ensuring the Internet's universality and openness for the future (No. 4), the Council of Europe Strategy aims at setting out a coherent vision for a sustainable long-term approach to the Internet whose success will depend greatly on multistakeholder dialogue and support (Executive Summary).

Ethics in the Information Society: The Nine ´P´s (Global Ethics Network for Applied Ethics)

Highlighting the importance of participation being a fundamental value for the knowledge society (p. 9), the Discussion Paper requests governments to base copyright enforcement initiatives on multistakeholder processes (p. 19), urges regulators to consider participation in their media regulation (p. 23), and calls upon international regulatory bodies for the

Information Society to ensure a multistakeholder approach based on transparency, accountability, and representativeness (p. 25).

Montevideo Statement on the Future of Internet Cooperation (Conference Outcome)

The Statement calls for speeding up the globalization of ICANN and IANA functions in order to create an environment in which all stakeholders can participate on an equal footing.

Riga Guidelines on Ethics in the Information Society (Conference Outcome)

The Guidelines encourage the participation of small islands and developing states, indigenous peoples, persons with disabilities and other marginalized users in the debates on the ethical challenges of the Information Society (Guidelines No. 2). The Guidelines emphasize the need to raise awareness of the importance of life-long education initiatives to equip all citizens with the skills and competences to participate actively in the Internet (Guideline No. 4), and to support the equitable participation of all stakeholders from all regions of the world (Guideline No. 5).The Guidelines also refer to the importance of strengthening policy-makers' ability to identify and remove barriers as to ensure the participation of all individuals in the Internet (Guidelines No. 9), and they support the promotion of broad-based multi-stakeholder partnerships aimed at addressing social cohesion and digital solidarity through the advocacy of human rights (Guideline No. 14).

Seoul Framework for and Commitment to Open and Secure Cyberspace (Conference Outcome)

The attainment of economic growth and development requires collaboration with multiple stakeholders including international organizations and the private sector (p. 1). Concerning capacity building, the Framework refers to the importance of having the full participation of governments, business, and civil society (p. 4).

Final Statement: Information and Knowledge for all (WSIS+10)

The Final Statement acknowledges that multistakeholder processes have become an essential approach in addressing issues affecting today's knowledge and information societies (p. 2). It invites all stakeholders to enhance the participation of young people and their access to the information revolution's benefits as key priorities (p. 3), and to coordinate as well as cooperate in a multistakeholder and inclusive manner at regional and international level for ensuring that the appropriate enabling environment is created for the further development of the ICT ecosystem (p. 4).

OECD Principles for Internet Policy Making

Dealing with multistakeholder cooperation in policy development processes, the OECD's fifth principle recognizes that the multistakeholder environment has underpinned the Internet governance process and the critical resources of management (Principle No. 5, pp. 8, 23). Thus, for strengthening Internet governance and achieving international public policy goals, governments are requested to apply a multistakeholder process (Principle No. 5, pp. 8, 23).

Communication on Internet Policy and Governance (European Commission)

Stating that debates about the strengthening of the Internet's multistakeholder governance have intensified in the recent past, the Communication proposes a basis for a common

European vision for Internet Governance in order to defend and promote multistakeholder governance structures based on rules respecting fundamental rights and democratic values (pp. 2, 4). In this respect, the European Commission argues in support of a genuine multistakeholder model taking decisions on the basis of principles of good governance, transparency, accountability, and the inclusiveness of all relevant stakeholders (pp. 3, 6). For strengthening the multistakeholder model, the Commission calls on all stakeholders to engage in capacity building for establishing and promoting multistakeholder processes, especially with regard to regions where such processes are less developed (p. 8).

Delhi Declaration for a Just and Equitable Internet (Conference Outcome)

Stating that the Internet needs to be maintained as a public space being available to all people (Principles Nos. 2, 13) and that the existing governance arrangements for the Internet are lacking democratic mechanisms, the Declaration calls for fundamental changes especially with regard to the establishment of effective participatory processes (Principles Nos. 1, 18).

Recommendation on a Guide to Human Rights for Internet Users (CoE)

Stating that all users (including children and young people) should be empowered to use the Internet for participating in democratic life (Recommendation No. 4; Children and young people No. 1), the Guide entitles Internet users to participate in local, national, and global public policy debates, legislative initiatives and public examination of decision-making processes (Assembly, association and participation, No. 3; Children and young people No. 1).

NETmundial Multistakeholder Statement (Conference Outcome)

Examining multistakeholder issues in great detail, the Statement's first Internet Governance process principle (Multistakeholder) acknowledges that the Internet should be built on democratic multistakeholder processes as to ensure the meaningful and accountable participation of all interested stakeholders, including governments, the private sector, civil society, the technical community, the academic community and the Internet users; the respective stakeholders' roles and responsibilities should be interpreted in a flexible manner depending on the issue in discussion (Internet Governance Principle No. 1). Furthermore, decision-making procedures must be developed and agreed upon through multistakeholder processes (Internet Governance Process Principles). Encompassing a number of issues deserving the attention of all stakeholders, the Statement's Roadmap observes that certain Internet Governance decisions are partly taken without all stakeholders' meaningful participation (Roadmap I.1). Accordingly, the improvement of multistakeholder decision-making is needed (Roadmap I.1), for instance by selecting stakeholder representatives through open, democratic, and transparent processes (Roadmap I.3). Multistakeholder mechanisms need to be developed at the national level since a number of Internet Governance issues should be managed at this level (Roadmap I. 4).

Paris Declaration (UNESCO)

The Declaration does not mention the term "multistakeholder" but addresses public participation (p. 1) and the importance of men and women having the right to equal right to participate in the media (p. 2).

EU Human Rights Guidelines on Freedom of Expression Online and Offline (Council of the European Union)

The European Union will continue its work towards maintaining and strengthening the Internet Governance's multistakeholder model (No. 33.f) and requests the European External Action Service (EEAS) and the European Commission services to actively engage in the IGF debates with a view to promoting a multistakeholder model (No. 56). Beyond that, the Guidelines refer to the important impact of technological innovations in ICT on the participation and contribution of citizens in decision-making processes (No. 6).

Towards a Collaborative, Decentralized Internet Governance Ecosystem (Panel Report)

The Panel's Report contains a number of recommendations for achieving a developed, collaborative, and decentralized Internet Governance ecosystem covering inter alia the support of broad multistakeholder alliances (p. 3). By adopting the Internet Governance principles produced in the *NETmundial Multistakeholder Statement*, the Panel shares the Statement's objectives and thus also the (above already described) assessment of multistakeholder participation within the Internet.

African Union Convention on Cyber Security and Personal Data Protection

Without discussing multistakeholder participation in detail, the Convention, in the context of cybersecurity governance, calls for encouraging the private sector to participate in government-led initiatives promoting cybersecurity (p. 29).

Lyon Declaration on Access to Information and Development (Conference Outcome)

The Declaration states that sustainable development must take place in a framework based on public participation of all interested stakeholders (Declaration No. 2.e), and asks for the provision of public fora for better civil society participation and engagement in decision-making (Declaration No. 4.e).

African Declaration on Internet Rights and Freedoms (Pan African Initiative)

Referring to the importance of improving multistakeholder decision-making and policy development at the national level for ensuring the full participation of all interested parties in the Internet, the Declaration suggests establishing independent multistakeholder bodies (Democratic Internet Governance Framework) and requests the technical communities to engage actively in the multistakeholder processes dealing with human rights and Internet Governance in Africa and to ensure Africa's participation in the development of open standards (Technical Communities). The Declaration also prompts Africa's academic institutions to promote and participate in the reinforcement of the continent's capacity in order to actively participate within the Internet development and policy fora.

Bali Road Map (Global Media Forum)

After recognizing that a sustainable development is subject to the participation of informed people (Preamble), the Road Map invites governments to ensure equal participation in the Internet for men and women (Governments, No. 5) and asks media professionals and social media users to promote gender-sensitive policies and strategies for supporting the participation of women and marginalised groups on all levels of media (Media outlets, media professionals and social media users, No. 5).

Nairobi Declaration on the Post 2015 Development Agenda (Global Forum for Media Development)
The Declaration does not address multistakeholder aspects in detail but notes that a sustainable development depends on the participation of informed people in governance processes and decision-making (Observations).

3.6.2 Conclusion

About 75 percent of the reviewed documents address participation and the majority of those use also the term multistakeholder participation. Generally, the documents acknowledge that online participation of all stakeholders involved is of importance. However, the propositions for actual multistakeholder processes mostly remain relatively vague. Only in recent years, the declarations, guidelines, and frameworks started to consider multistakeholder participation in more detail; even if the contours of possible models are not yet clear and the terminology is not settled, the key message can be seen in the need to increase the participation of more societal voices. Correspondingly, civil society and its organizations will be confronted with new implications, for example related to procedural issues in the decision-building approaches. For example: How to define certain groups such as academia or technical community? Who is entitled to speak on behalf of a group?

For obvious reasons, cultural and contextual factors play an important role in shaping the functioning and the outcome of multistakeholder processes. The way of seeking legitimacy is also different (voting processes, checks and balances, etc.). Usually, the composition of the participants is a key element and also influences a variety of complex issues, for example the communications, the decision-making procedures and the conflicts' resolutions. In a number of documents it seems to be generally accepted that the main success factors for multistakeholder participation are transparency, accountability and inclusiveness. However, most of the statements considered are lacking an extensive analysis of the different facets of multistakeholderism.

The documents addressing multistakeholder participation encompass the main pillars of the "Internet Universality" concept as follows: About 70 percent also address accessibility and half of the documents address openness. As regards rights, 60 percent discuss freedom of expression and a little more than 50 percent deal with privacy issues.

3.7 Gender Equality

3.7.1 Contents of Documents

Only 18 of the 52 reviewed texts deal with gender equality, among them six Declarations. Within these reviewed documents, the first reference to gender equality is contained in the Geneva Declaration of Principles and the Geneva Plan of Action, both published on 12 December 2003.

Geneva Declaration of Principles/Geneva Plan of Action
With reference to the Declaration's challenge of harnessing the full potential of the ICT to promote the development goals of the Millennium Declaration, the promotion of gender equality and empowerment of women is addressed (No. 2). By affirming that the development of ICT provides enormous opportunities for women, who should be an

essential part of, and key actors in, the Information Society, the Declaration commits itself to ensure that the Information Society enables women's empowerment and their full participation on the basis of equality in all spheres of society and in all decisionmaking processes by mainstreaming a gender equality perspective (No. 12).

Regarding the implementation of gender mainstreaming, the Geneva Plan of Action outlines a number of suggestions, in particular in the context of capacity building, eemployment and cultural as well as linguistic diversity. For enabling all, especially girls and women, to benefit from the Information Society, the Plan of Action urges removing the gender barriers to ICT education by, among others, establishing early intervention programmes in science and technology (No. 11.g). Furthermore, the development of best practices for e-employers based on gender equality should be supported (No. 19). In the context of cultural and linguistic diversity, the document suggests strengthening programmes focused on gender-sensitive curricula in formal and non-formal education for all, and enhancing communication and media literacy for women with a view to building the capacity of girls and women to understand and to develop ICT content (No. 23.h).

Tunis Agenda for the Information Society (WSIS)

The Agenda emphasizes the importance of building ICT capacity and confidence in the use of ICT by all for achieving internationally agreed development goals and objectives (No. 90). For achieving gender equality, the Tunis Agenda proposes effective training and education that motivates and promotes participation and active involvement of girls and women in the decision-making process of building the Information Society (No. 90).

APC Internet Rights Charter

By pointing to the fact that women and men often are not given the same opportunities, the APC Internet Rights Charter emphasizes the importance of having the right of equal access to the Internet for men and women for learning about, defining, accessing, using and shaping the Internet regardless of gender (No. 1.5). It may be noted here that APC in 2014 also produced Feminist Principles of the Internet.[71]

Tshwane Declaration on Information Ethics in Africa (Conference Outcome)

According to the Tshwane Declaration on Information Ethics in Africa, all information should be made available, accessible and affordable across all gender.

Final Recommendations of the European Conference on "Ethics and Human Rights in the Information Society"

With regard to the development and implementation of a policy regulating universal access to the Internet, the Recommendations state that an effective access policy should be inspired by ethical values of solidarity and social justice irrespective of (among others) the Internet users' gender (No. 14).

Reflection and Analysis by UNESCO on the Internet

Addressing gender equality as being one of UNESCO's global priorities, and with regard to the still existing digital divide across gender, this document proposes genderresponsive toolkits and methodologies empowering policy-makers and others to adopt measures suited to their local environments (Nos. 2, 39, 41).

---

71   http://www.genderit.org/articles/feminist-principles-internet.

African Platform on Access to Information Declaration (Conference Outcome)

By acknowledging that access to information is of fundamental importance to fostering gender equality (p. 1), the African Platform on Access to Information Declaration addresses the issue repeatedly. Initially, the declaration's first Key Principle states that access to information should be open to everyone regardless of his or her gender (p. 2). For achieving this goal, governments, civil society and the media shall be obligated to facilitate women's and girls' access to information for enabling them to participate in public life and defend their own rights. Furthermore, the declaration asks civil society organizations to make the best use of access to information mechanisms to monitor governments' fulfilment of commitments for promoting gender equality and ensuring that the delivery of services targeted at women will be enhanced. In addition, the collection, management and release of information should be gender disaggregated (Application of Principles No. 4). The Pan African Conference on Access to Information also calls on all media to recognize and be responsive to gender differences (p. 8).

Council of Europe and Internet: Maximizing Rights, Minimizing Restrictions

With regard to gender equality, the document refers to the Council of Europe's Convention on Preventing and Combating Violence against Women and Domestic Violence of 12 April 2011,[72] highlighting the role of the communication technologies sector and the media in contributing to the prevention of violence and to the enhancement of respect for the dignity of women.

Ethics in the Information Society: The Nine P's (Global Ethics Network for Applied Ethics)

The Globethics.net Foundation deems information, communication and knowledge as being key drivers of development in globalized, multicultural, knowledge-based societies. Accordingly, a future knowledge society should be value-based, people-centred, communities and identities-oriented, education-focused, generation-oriented and, moreover, gender-oriented. Concerning the gender aspect, the Discussion Paper emphasizes gender equality in access to information, communication, knowledge and decision-making as being an important dimension of an inclusive and people-centred society. This also includes women's representation and participation in the ICT's decision-making processes (pp. 12/13). To achieve these objectives, Globethics.net requests to fully integrate gender analysis and principles in WSIS-related strategies and to facilitate their implementation (p. 28).

Final Statement: Information and Knowledge for all (WSIS+10)

The Final Statement invites all stakeholders to fully integrate gender equality perspectives in WSIS-related strategies and facilitate their implementation (p. 3). For achieving gender equality, women's innovative and meaningful use of ICTs should be advanced (p. 3).

NETmundial Multistakeholder Statement (Conference Outcome)

The NETmundial *Roadmap for the future evolution of the Internet Governance Ecosystem* urges meaningful participation of all interested parties in the Internet Governance discussions and the decision-making within the World Wide Web having regard to geographic, stakeholder and gender balances in order to avoid asymmetries (Roadmap 2.I.5).[73]

---

72   See http://www.conventions.coe.int/Treaty/EN/Treaties/Html/210.htm.
73   By recognizing, fully supporting, and adopting the IG Principles produced in the NETmundial Multistakeholder Statement the Report Towards a Collaborative, Decentralized Internet Governance

Paris Declaration (UNESCO)

Without addressing gender equality in detail, the Declaration emphasizes that both men and women have the right to equal access to and participate in the media (p. 2).

EU Human Rights Guidelines on Freedom of Expression Online and Offline (Council of the European Union)

There is no explicit reference to the terms gender and gender equality within the document. However, the Guidelines' general considerations point to the fact that full use will be made of existing and applicable EU human rights guidelines. By pointing to the *EU guidelines on violence against women and girls and combating all forms of discrimination* that among others promote gender equality[74], these issues are indirectly addressed (No. 26). For securing gender equality, the Guidelines' implementation and evaluation will be evaluated by a number of organizations including women's organizations (No. 71).

Lyon Declaration on Access to Information and Development (Conference Outcome)

Taking the view that increasing access to information and knowledge across society, assisted by the availability of ICT, supports sustainable development and improves people's lives, the *Lyon Declaration on Access to Information and Development* recognizes that sustainable development must take place in a human-rights based framework that among others empowers and educates marginalized groups including women (Declaration No. 2.a). For enhancing gender equality and therewith women's social, economic and political engagement, access to education is of utmost importance (Declaration No. 2.b).

African Declaration on Internet Rights and Freedoms (Pan African Initiative)

Stating that the Internet is an enabling space and resource for the realization of all human rights, the *African Declaration on Internet Rights and Freedoms* contains 12 Internet Principles including the right of all people to use the Internet as part of their right to dignity and for participating in social and cultural life (Marginalized groups, Principle No. 10). States as well as non-state actors should respect and protect the rights of all people to use the Internet by paying special attention to the needs of marginalized groups. For realizing gender equality and entitling women and men to equal access in order to learn about, define, use, and shape the Internet, all forms of discrimination against women need to be eliminated by analyzing and redressing the existing gender inequality. Policies and strategies must address cultural religious, social, economic and educational barriers. Internet content has to reflect women's needs. For achieving gender equality, processes and mechanisms enabling the full, active and equal participation of women and girls in the Internet should be developed and strengthened.

Bali Road Map (Global Media Forum)

For achieving gender equality, the participants of the Global Media Forum invite governments to ensure equal access and participation for men and women as regards the Internet and other ICT. The map also urges equal access in media ownership and decision-making, and support for the coverage of gender equality issues as being an essential part of development (Governments, Nos. 5, 6).

Ecosystem by the Panel on Global Internet Cooperation and Governance Mechanisms is also emphasizing the importance of a gender balance in the future evolution of Internet Governance (pp. 6, 36).

74   EU guidelines on violence against women and girls and combating all forms of discrimination, 8. December 2008, at p. 2, available at: <http://www.consilium.europa.eu/uedocs/cmsUpload/16173cor.en08.pdf>.

3.7.2 Conclusion

Most of the documents dealing with gender equality refer to the fact that access to the Internet should be available for all regardless of the gender. Particular attention has, however, been given to gender issues in a specific declaration referred to above, namely the Feminist Principles for the Internet produced by the APC. But in view of the fact that the issue of gender equality has only been occasionally addressed within the reviewed declarations, guidelines and frameworks, to date the issue can be said to have generally received little attention.

3.8 Sustainable Development

3.8.1 Contents of Documents

Substantial attention is given to the issue of supporting sustainable development; almost 50 percent (24 out of 52) of the declarations, guidelines and frameworks deal with that issue in one aspect or another.

SADC Declaration on Information and Communications Technology
The SADC Declaration aims at enhancing the standard and quality of peoples' life in Southern Africa by supporting sustainable development and economic growth and thereby reducing poverty (SADC Objectives).

Geneva Declaration of Principles/Geneva Plan of Action
Stating that a well-developed information and communication network infrastructure helps to promote sustainable economic progress of both developed and developing countries (B2)22.; B6)41.), the Declaration proposes building confidence and security in the use of ICT, (B5)35.) and maximizing economic benefits by governments intervening in order to correct failures, to maintain fair competition and to enhance the ICT infrastructure's development (B6)39.). Furthermore, economic development will be encouraged by the development of local content suited to domestic or regional needs (B8)53.).

With regard to e-commerce, the *Geneva Plan of Action* suggests that governments act as model users and early adopters in accordance with their level of socio-economic development (C6.13.n.). For stimulating sustainable economic growth, government policies should favor assistance to small and medium-sized enterprises in the ICT industry (C7.16.c.).

Tunis Agenda for the Information Society (WSIS)
The Agenda highlights the importance of achieving sustainable development and recognizes the role of ICT for achieving economic growth and development (Nos. 90, 91).

APC Internet Rights Charter
The Charter, demanding an Internet for social justice and sustainable development, highlights the Internet, in particular its neutrality, as being an important factor for economic development (No. 6.6).

Tshwane Declaration on Information Ethics in Africa (Conference Outcome)

Even though there is no explicit reference to the promotion of economic growth within the Declaration, the signatories attach great importance to the fact that ethics in the Internet should play a crucial role in African education and policy in order to foster sustainable development (Preamble).

Seoul Declaration for the Future of the Internet Economy (OECD)

With reference to the necessity of promoting the Internet economy and therewith sustainably stimulating economic growth (p. 4), the signatories of the Seoul Declaration agree to ensure that the Internet Economy is truly global by adopting policies that recognize the importance of a competitive environment for its successful growth (p. 8). By referring to the OECD's Report on *Shaping Policies for the Future of the Internet Economy* of 18 June 2008,[75] the signatories invite the organization to analyze the Internet Economy's future development (p. 9).

Code of Good Practice on Information, Participation and Transparency in Internet Governance (CoE, UNECE, APC)

By pointing to the Internet's growing importance, the Code of Good Practice refers to the Internet's impact on the economy; in this respect the Code emphasizes the importance of involving stakeholders with economic experience in the Internet's development (p. 3).

Asia Declaration on Internet Governance (Centre for Policy Initiatives)

Access to (and use of) the Internet make an important contribution to a country's (sustainable) economic development (Key Observation No. 1). Conversely, a country's economic development can also have an effect on whether and how often people can access the Internet (Key Observation No. 1).

Reflection and Analysis by UNESCO on the Internet

Highlighting sustainable development as one of UNESCO's "overarching objectives" (No. 41), the report refers to the importance of adopting ethical Internet standards and to the role of digital heritage in sustainable development (Nos. 16, 19).

Promotion, protection and enjoyment of human rights on the Internet (Human Rights Council)

The document does not address the term "sustainable development" in detail, but refers to the Internet's open nature as being an important tool for achieving development in its various forms (Nos. 2, 5).

Seoul Framework for and Commitment to Open and Secure Cyberspace (Conference Outcome)

Examining sustainable economic growth and development in some detail, the Seoul Framework refers to the Internet's importance to preserve an open environment that supports innovation, entrepreneurship and business transformation, as well as empowers Internet users in online transactions and exchanges (p. 1). In order to promote economic development and growth, the access to and use of broadband Internet networks worldwide needs to be improved (p. 1).

---

75 See http://www.oecd.org/sti/40821707.pdf.

Final Statement: Information and Knowledge for all (WSIS+10)

The Final Statement considers education and scientific knowledge as being key factors for achieving sustainable development and peace, and invites all stakeholders to build sustainable knowledge societies (pp. 2, 3).

OECD Principles for Internet Policy Making

The document does not explicitly deal with economic development. However, in connection with the promotion of the open, distributed and interconnected nature of the Internet, attention is drawn to the fact that the Internet's openness has played a major role in its success in fostering economic growth (Principle No. 2, p. 6). Stating that high speed networks and services are crucial for future economic growth, a robust competition in high speed broadband Internet is requested (Principle No. 3, p. 7).

Communication on Internet Policy and Governance (European Commission)

Although not explicitly addressing economic development, the Communication rates the Internet as being a fundamental pillar of the Digital Single Market, among others having fostered innovation, economic growth, and trade (p. 2). Furthermore, the Communication considers confidence in the Internet and its governance as being an important prerequisite for unlocking the Internet's potential as an engine for economic growth and innovation (p. 9).

Delhi Declaration for a Just and Equitable Internet (Conference Outcome)

Recalling that the Internet can be seen as a breeding ground for new models of economic activity (Principle No. 1) and that both the Internet and the digital economy have become key elements for the overall economy, the Declaration calls for measures to be taken to ensure economic justice and economic development (Principle No. 6).

NETmundial Multistakeholder Statement (Conference Outcome)

According to the NETmundial Statement's principle on "Protection of Intermediaries", intermediary liability limitations should be implemented in a way that respects and promotes economic growth and innovation (Internet Governance Principles).[76]

EU Human Rights Guidelines on Freedom of Expression Online and Offline (Council of the European Union)

Rating ICT as being part of everyday life that provides new opportunities for the fulfilment of human rights and for social and economic development (No. 33), the Guidelines seek to ensure that the Internet and other ICT remain a driver of economic growth. As to that, the European External Action Service (EEAS) and the Commission services should build on existing actions such as the "No Disconnect Strategy" (No. 48).

Paris Declaration (UNESCO)

Addressing sustainable development at various places, the Declaration refers to the importance of free expression for governance to achieve sustainable development (p. 2).

---

[76] The same applies for the report of the Panel on Global Internet Co-operation and Goverance Mechanisms, Towards a Collaborative, Decentralized Internet Goverance Ecosystem.

Lyon Declaration on Access to Information and Development (Conference Outcome)

The Declaration does not explicitly mention the term "economic development". Nevertheless, it indirectly refers to this issue's importance by pointing to how access to information empowers people to be economically active, productive and innovative (Principles).

African Declaration on Internet Rights and Freedoms (Pan African Initiative)

With reference to the Internet's influence on the (sustainable) economic development in Africa (Preamble), the Declaration's Key Principle No. 7 points to the importance of a right to development. This principle's implementation requires the promotion of media and information literacy for ensuring that consumers of media products have the ability to find, evaluate, and engage with various types of information, including those relevant for economic development. Accordingly, ICT should be designed, developed and implemented in a manner that contributes to sustainable human development and empowerment.

Bali Road Map (Global Media Forum)

The Road Map realizes the media's potential to contribute to sustainable development; in that regard, the participants of the Global Media Forum invite UNESCO and the international community to promote greater understanding about the importance of freedom of expression and to support independent media to play their full role in sustainable development (UNESCO and the international community, Nos. 2, 3)

Nairobi Declaration on the Post 2015 Development Agenda (Global Forum for Media Development)

The Declaration refers to the fact that sustainable development depends on the informed participation of people in governance processes and decision-making (Observations).

3.8.2 Conclusion

Summarizing, it can be said that, to date, sustainable economic development related to the Internet has not received major attention. To the extent that the issue is mentioned within the reviewed documents, the wording is limited to vague statements like that the Internet's openness and neutrality play a major role for its success in fostering economic growth. Real suggestions on how the Internet can contribute to sustainable development, including the environmental dimension to improve the (sustainable) economic development, are not available even if the right to development is stated (such as in the mentioned IRPC Charter).

3.9 Issues of Culture, Science and the Social and Human Sciences, and Education

3.9.1 Cultural Diversity

Only 20 of the 52 reviewed documents address cultural issues;[77] furthermore, most of them only mention the term culture or a related term.

Documents mentioning cultural issues without any detailed discussion are the UNESCO's *Recommendation on the Promotion and Use of Multilingualism and Universal Access to*

---

77 In addition, the IRPC Charter addresses the right to culture in parallel to the right of access to knowledge (Article 11).

Cyberspace, the *Tunis Agenda for the Information Society*, the *Seoul Declaration for the Future of the Internet Economy*, the *Committee of Minister's Declaration on Internet Governance Principles*, the *Riga Guidelines on Ethics in the Information Society*, the *Joint Declaration on Universality and the Right to Freedom of Expression*, the *Delhi Declaration for a Just and Equitable Internet*, the *NETmundial Multistakeholder Statement*, the *Report by the Panel on Global Internet Cooperation and Governance Mechanisms Towards a Collaborative, Decentralized Internet Governance Ecosystem*, the UNESCO's *Paris Declaration*, the *EU Human Rights Guidelines on Freedom of Expression Online and Offline* and the *Lyon Declaration on Access to Information and Development*.

In eight of the 52 reviewed documents, cultural aspects are addressed and concretized in more detail.

By way of example, the *Geneva Declaration of Principles* highlights cultural diversity of being the "common heritage of humankind" on which the Information Society should be founded (No. 52). The Declaration also suggests preserving cultural heritage for the future, to the benefit of individuals remembering where the society was coming from (No. 54). The *Geneva Plan of Action* complements the Declaration's remarks by suggesting policies that support the respect and enhancement of cultural diversity and by developing local cultural industries suited to the Internet users' cultural context (No. 23.a). In addition, the Plan of Action argues in favor of supporting efforts to develop as well as use ICT for the cultural heritage's preservation (No. 23.c).

Within the context of promoting the expression of all cultures on the Internet (Recommendation No. 18), the *Final Recommendations of the European Conference on "Ethics and Human Rights in the Information Society"* propose the extension of the UNESCO's 2005 Convention on the Protection and Promotion of the Diversity of Cultural Expressions[78] for encouraging both individuals and cultural communities to create cultural goods and have access to their own cultural expressions in order to make the Internet a common place for all different cultures.

The document *Reflection and Analysis by UNESCO on the Internet* discusses cultural heritage in more detail (Nos. 17, 18, 19, 38).

Stating that all cultures can contribute to global values, the Discussion Paper on *Ethics in the Information Society: The Nine 'P's*[79] calls upon governments, content producers, media owners and consumers to ensure "cultural diversity" (pp. 13, 15, 28).

By repeating the Geneva Declaration of Principles' wording, the *Seoul Framework for and Commitment to Open and Secure Cyberspace*[80] rates cultural diversity as being the common heritage of humankind, and seeks to promote respect for cultural identity as well as cultural diversity (p. 2).

By stating that knowledge societies should seek to ensure full respect for cultural diversity (p. 2) the WSIS+10 Review Event's *Final Statement: Information and Knowledge for all (WSIS+10)* invites all stakeholders to respect cultural diversity and keep in mind that cultural expressions and enhanced cultural diversity are essential for progress towards inclusive knowledge societies (p. 3).

---

78   See http://portal.unesco.org/en/ev.php-URL_ID=31038&URL_DO=DO_TOPIC&URL_SECTION=201.html.
79   Released by the Global Ethics Network for Applied Ethics.
80   Outcome of the 2013 Seoul Conference on Cyberspace.

Dealing with cultural and linguistic diversity, the *African Declaration on Internet Rights and Freedoms*'[81] sixth Key Principle emphasizes the importance of cultural diversity for the society's development and calls for the protection of Africa's cultural diversity. It adds that the creation of varied information and the digitalization of educational, scientific and cultural heritage are needed. Advocating for all stakeholders to take action towards the realization of the rights and principles set in the Declaration, UNESCO is explicitly asked to integrate the African Declaration on Internet Rights and Freedoms into its "Priority Africa" strategies and to promote the advancement of cultural rights on the Internet.

3.9.2 Science

Only 6 of the 52 reviewed documents address science issues, namely the Max Planck Society's *Berlin Declaration on Open Access to Knowledge in the Sciences and Humanities*, the *Geneva Declaration of Principles* and the *Geneva Plan of Action*, the WSIS *Tunis Agenda for the Information Society*, the *Reflection and Analysis by UNESCO on the Internet* and the WSIS+10 *Final Statement: Information and Knowledge for all*.

In this regard, the following issues, among others, were raised: promotion of new open access paradigms to gain the most benefits for science and society (Berlin Declaration, p. 2); the role of science within the Information Society's development (Geneva Declaration of Principles, Nos. 7, 26); the introduction of early intervention programs in science and technology for girls to increase the number of women in ICT careers (Geneva Plan of Action, No. 11.g); as well as the correlation between ICT applications and sustainable development in the field of science within the framework of national e-strategies (Geneva Plan of Action, No. 14).

Also addressed are: the collaboration in science and technology (Tunis Agenda, No. 90); ethics training for science journalists (Reflection and Analysis by UNESCO on the Internet, No. 11), human science knowledge (Reflection and Analysis by UNESCO on the Internet, Nos. 12, 14, 15); as well as the importance of sharing the public good science (Final Statement: Information and Knowledge for all, p. 2).

3.9.3 Education

About 40 percent of the declarations, guidelines and frameworks reviewed (24 out of 52) mention educational aspects.[82] However, half of the references are more or less limited to the term education, i.e. detailed considerations are missing. This is the case in the *APC Internet Rights Charter*, the *Maputo Declaration*, the *Seoul Declaration for the Future of the Internet Economy*, the *Joint Declaration on Freedom of Expression and the Internet*, the *Internet Governance Council of Europe Strategy 2012-2015*, the *Council of Europe and Internet: Maximizing Rights, Minimizing Restrictions*, the *Recommendation of the Council concerning Guidelines governing the Protection of Privacy and Transborder Flows of Personal Data*, the *Riga Guidelines on Ethics in the Information Society*, the *EU Human Rights Guidelines on Freedom of Expression Online and Offline*, the Report by the Panel on Global Internet Cooperation and Governance Mechanisms *Towards a Collaborative, Decentralized Internet Governance Ecosystem* and the *Lyon Declaration on Access to Information and Development*.

---

81 Released by the Pan African Initiative to promote human rights standards and principles of openness.
82 In addition, the IRPC Charter addresses education as an important topic in its Article 10.

Merely 13 of the 52 reviewed documents deal with education and educational issues in more detail.

In so doing, UNESCO's Recommendation on the Promotion and Use of Multilingualism and Universal Access to Cyberspace recognizes that basic education must be seen as a prerequisite for universal access to cyberspace (Preamble). Accordingly, UNESCO recommends the public and private sector and the civil society encourage the creation and processing of, and access to, educational content (Rec. No. 1), and invites Member States and international organizations to develop "human capital" for the information society, including an open, integrated and intercultural education combined with ICT skills training (Rec. No. 19).

The Geneva Declaration of Principles states that the sharing and strengthening of global knowledge for development can be enhanced by removing barriers to equitable access to education (No. 25.). It also states that universal primary education works as a key factor for building a fully inclusive information society (No. 29.), and it promotes the use of ICT in education (No. 30).

According to the Geneva Plan of Action, ICT can contribute to achieving universal education worldwide through, among others, delivery of education and training of teachers (No. 11). The Plan asks for the provision of Internet users with the necessary knowledge and skills to apply ICT (No. 11.d), and works on removing existing gender barriers to ICT (No. 11.g). For building confidence and security in the use of ICT, governments, in cooperation with the private sector, are asked to detect cybercrime and respond to the misuse of ICT. Governments and other stakeholders are also urged to promote user education and awareness about online privacy (No. 12 b, c).

In the context of the right to education, the *Declaration of the Committee of Ministers on Human Rights and the Rule of Law in the Information Society* asks Member States to facilitate access to ICT devices and to promote education for allowing everybody to acquire the necessary skills for working with a broad range of ICTs (I.3.).

The *Tunis Agenda for the Information Society* (WSIS) refers to the importance of building ICT capacity of all through the improvement and delivery of relevant education and training programmes enabling lifelong and distance learning. In that regard, the Tunis Agenda relates in particular to the participation and active involvement of girls and women (No. 90). Furthermore, the Tunis Agenda promotes the use of media as educational and learning tools (No. 90).

Comprising a right to access to knowledge (No. 3.1) and a right to education (No. 7.1), the *APC Internet Rights Charter*, asks governing bodies to make freely available all information about rights and procedures related to the Internet, as for instance the Internet users' rights or mechanisms to address rights violations (No. 7.1).

The document on *Reflection and Analysis by UNESCO on the Internet* refers to UNESCO's core mandate in building peace in the minds of all men and women through inter alia education and the sciences (No. 4). In that regard, the Organization is of the opinion that the Internet can enhance education through a variety of means, including open and distance learning as soon as the barriers to access the Internet are overcome (No. 6).

Stating that access to education depends on the granting of access to information (Preamble), the *African Platform on Access to Information Declaration*[83] refers to governments'

---

83 Outcome of the Pan African Conference on Access to Information.

duty to make information about educational policies and assessments of their impact publicly available (Application of Principles No. 7).

The document *Ethics in the Information Society: The Nine P's*[84] rates access to education as being a basic right and public good (p. 10). Mainly dealing with educational aspects within the context of "People" (the third "P"), the Discussion Paper states that a knowledge society should be education-focused and therefore calls upon educational institutions to increase information ethics in the curricula (pp. 12/13).

The Council of Europe's *Recommendation on a Guide to Human Rights for Internet Users* recognizes the right to education, including access to information (Education and literacy). This right covers inter alia online access to education in general, and access to digital education and knowledge for exercising own rights. For protecting children and young people from any interference with their physical, mental or moral welfare online, they shall be provided with education to protect themselves (Children and young people).

The *Final Statement: Information and Knowledge for all* (WSIS+10) considers education that reaches out to all members of society, and which provides lifelong learning opportunities, as being the key to empowering people for sustainable development and peace (p. 2). Accordingly, all stakeholders are invited to support the provision of granting all equal access to education, science and technology (p. 3).

Without addressing education in detail, the *African Union Convention on Cyber Security and Personal Data Protection*, under the heading "Education and training", calls for the adoption of measures to develop capacity building for different stakeholders covering all areas of cybersecurity (p. 28).

For realizing its declared ten Key Principles (for instance Internet access, right to information and online privacy), the *African Declaration on Internet Rights and Freedoms*[85] refers to a number of requirements, among them "Access to Knowledge and Education". In that regard, the Declaration states that media and information literacy must be promoted for enabling all interested people to access the Internet, to interpret the contents that may be found there and to make informed judgments as users of information.

4. Relevance for UNESCO

4.1 Findings of the Documents' Analysis

4.1.1 Compatibility and Completeness of Existing Documents

The above analysis of the compatibility and completeness of declarations, guidelines, and frameworks containing Internet Governance principles has shown that a large number of corresponding documents have been developed and implemented during the last 25 years. However, these documents are rather disparate and mainly reflect the requirements applicable in a given historical environment. If a special organization or a group of special organizations have been interested in implementing certain Internet Governance principles, the respective initiative was taken and the developed document approved by the involved participants.

---

84 Released by the Global Ethics Network for Applied Ethics.
85 Released by the Pan African Initiative to promote human rights standards and principles of openness.

Due to the different political, economic, and social background of the developed declarations, guidelines, and frameworks, the development of a clear and coherent normative structure is still in its infancy. This fact is insofar not surprising as the historical and cultural environment has a major impact on the respective documents. This environment is manifold since – indeed positively – the geographic origin of the documents is rather broad, i.e. not only the traditional developed countries have proceeded with attempts to state Internet Governance principles. Notwithstanding the comparability of those declarations, guidelines, and frameworks that encompass similar principles, however, direct relations between the documents have generally not been established.

The overall trend is not only one of disparities however, because there are signs of shared normative elements in regard to many issues. What the overall picture does illustrate, however, is that = there is no single existing document that covers all the Organization's specific needs concerning principles that apply to its areas of interest in the Internet.

Combining this assessment with the "Internet Universality" concept and the R.O.A.M. framework (meaning the four principles of human rights, openness, accessible for all and multistakeholder participation), the following conclusions may be relevant for consideration:

- The element of *human rights* (particularly freedom of expression and privacy) is quite well covered in the existing declarations, guidelines, and frameworks. This analysis corresponds to the fact that international legal instruments encompassing human rights are available (on the global level by the United Nations, but also on the regional level for example in Europe), and that human rights are indivisible making it necessary to realize a more complete rather than a fragmented picture.

- The pillar of *technical and economic openness* has historically not been a main task of legislators and regulators but of engineers, technicians, intellectual property industries, etc. Open standards and open architecture are to the benefit of the whole society; therefore, these objectives are realized in the own interest of all infrastructure participants. Apart from technical issues, however, access to infrastructure and net neutrality have also become a legal debate in the recent past.[86] Openness has also been an issue concerning open access educational resources online. Access is a precondition for openness of information and communication channels constituting a genuine interest of the society. The links between access and openness in many documents correctly reflect the corresponding relations.

- *Accessiblity as social dimension* encompasses *inter alia* universal access, multilingualism, quality of content, and ethics. The existing documents are not very forthcoming in terms of dealing with these issues. Multilingualism and quality of content are hardly addressed in the existing documents. Universal access is seen more as a technical element than a social dimension.

- *Multistakeholder participation* was introduced in the Tunis Agenda; thereafter, multistakeholderism has slowly become a discussion topic but only gained major importance during the last three years. The NETmundial Conference in Sao Paulo, Brazil, in April 2014 is an example of a gathering trying to apply multistakeholder principles, thereby summarizing ten years of discussions. Notwithstanding this assessment, the treatment of multistakeholders still merits being elaborated in more depth.

---

86 In the UNESCO context see also MacKinnon et al., 2014, 78-80.

- Convincingly, *ethics* has become a more important dimension during the last few years but more emphasis could still be put on this.

Apart from the "Internet Universality" concept, additional indicators for the above analysis have been the objectives and priorities for UNESCO's general policies, namely freedom of expression, education, science, culture, gender equality, and sustainable development:

- *Freedom of expression* being part of the human rights is extensively addressed in the existing documents; as mentioned, human rights play a key role in the "Internet Universality" concept of UNESCO.

- *Education* supporting the building of knowledge societies is mentioned in several declarations, guidelines, and frameworks, but the degree of concretization of its contents has remained low. Education directly relates to freedom and human rights as well as the access and openness in the R.O.A.M. framework.

- *Science and the Social and Human Sciences* are only rarely mentioned in the reviewed documents and can also not be seen as issues which easily fit into the Internet Governance principles. Therefore, the fact that they are not frequently addressed in the examined documents corresponds to the different scope of their status. Nevertheless, the sciences exercises their function in connection with the technical/economic openness and with access and social inclusion issues as contained in the "Internet Universality" concept.

- *Culture* (intercultural dialogue, rapprochement) is an objective both embedded in the human rights understanding and in the social dimension of access as well as in the concept of multistakeholderism as part of the R.O.A.M. framework. With good reasons, culture is addressed in many declarations, guidelines, and frameworks; however, the respective statements remain relatively vague and abstain from proclaiming specific objectives.

- With the exception of the APC's "Feminist Principles of the Internet", gender equality in general only plays a minor role in the existing documents; this objective merits to be included into the multistakeholder approach contained in the R.O.A.M. framework.

- *Sustainable development* (incl. priority for Africa) can be found in a number of existing documents, but the inclusion of the respective aims has remained rather weak. Sustainability has also not been an important issue in the past.

The outlined assessment shows the need to better link the available Internet Governance principles with UNESCO's "Internet Universality" concept as well as to more strongly develop certain objectives and aims of UNESCO.

4.1.2 Normative character of existing documents

Assessing the legal quality of declarations, guidelines, and frameworks the conclusion must be drawn that most documents are not of a binding nature ("hard law") since these documents do not constitute multilateral treaties. However, in varying degrees they have a moral "force". Some may play a role as "soft law" which is more than "no law", even if a direct enforcement of the respective provisions is not possible.

Soft law can be considered as a social notion close to law covering certain forms of expected and acceptable codes of conduct. Based on this appreciation, scholars are attempting to build bridges in order to overcome the dichotomy between "hard law" and "soft law" as well as to attach hard sanctions to "soft law" in case of "non-compliance".[87]

Multilateral treaty negotiation processes are usually slow and tending to a low common denominator in the achieved results. Meanwhile, the rapid technological developments require the possibility to adapt normative frameworks in a timely way and therefore, declarations and guidelines from recognized international organizations can be considered as valuable influences in the rule-making environment.

Different levels of normative prescriptions may be distinguished.. Documents which have been developed between participants at a conference or similar events ending with ad hoc-statements or documents negotiated between a small number of participants usually have a limited moral or reputational impact. In contrast, if the originators of a document are established and esteemed international organizations (for example UNESCO, OECD, or the Council of Europe), the "normative" character of the declarations/recommendations might have a higher impact on the Member States of the respective organization. In addition, the institutional framework could increase the indirect incentive for Member States to comply with the respective principles.

4.1.3 Accountability mechanisms

As a consequence of the partly weak normative character of most of the existing declarations, guidelines, and frameworks, the accountability mechanisms have remained underdeveloped. Accountability as a term or notion is often mentioned in the existing documents, however, its content is only rarely discussed. A reason for this can be seen in the difficulty to establish enforcement measures applicable in case of non-compliance with the requested accountability task.

Accountability that could tackle apparent legitimacy problems is not necessarily strengthened by proposals to implement some kind of intergovernmental supervision. Typically, accountability is bolstered through measures of institutional checks and balances, an element which is missing in the existing documents. Furthermore, the hardest consequence of accountability, namely a mechanism of sanctions, is nowhere proposed in the existing documents. However, some documents (for example the Recommendation on a Guide to Human Rights for Internet Users of the Council of Europe and the IRPC Charter) do refer to a right to redress.

Not less 28 out of the 52 reviewed declarations, guidelines, and frameworks refer to the "accountability" principle. Looking at the chronology, accountability is addressed in the *Geneva Plan of Action* (2003) for the first time; since 2011, accountability can be found in almost all reviewed documents. This fact shows that accountability has recently become an important issue. Furthermore, most documents only refer to accountability without discussing its contents in detail.

The following declarations, guidelines, and frameworks briefly mention the accountability principle:

---

87 Weber, 2014, 26.

The 2003 *Geneva Plan of Action* (No. 15 (c)), the 2005 *Declarations of the Committee of Ministers on Human Rights and the Rule of Law in the Information Society* (No. 7, with additional reference to responsiveness), the 2006 *APC Internet Rights Charter* (No. 3.1), the 2008 *Maputo Declaration: Fostering Freedom of Expression, Access to Information and Empowerment of People*, the 2008 *Seoul Declaration for the Future of the Internet Economy* (pp. 5 and 6), the 2010 *Code of Good Practice on Information, Participation and Transparency in Internet Governance* (pp. 2 and 5), the 2011 launched *10 Internet Rights and Principles* (No. 10), the 2011 *Reflection and Analysis by UNESCO on the Internet* (p. 5), the 2011 *African Platform on Access to Information Declaration* (pp. 1, 5, 6, 8 and 9), the 2011 *Declaration by the Committee of Ministers on Internet Governance Principles* (Nos. 2 and 7), the 2012 *Internet Governance – Council of Europe Strategy 2012-2015* (No. 13 (d)), the 2013 *Ethics in the Information Society: The Nine 'P's* (pp. 9, 22 and 25, with additional reference to responsibility), the 2013 *Recommendation of the Council concerning Guidelines governing the Protection of Privacy and Transborder Flows of Personal Data* (with many references to accountability), the 2013 Riga Guidelines on Ethics in the Information Society (No. 3), the 2014 *OECD Principles of Internet Policy Making* (pp. 10 and 24), the 2014 by the European Commission proposed Communication on Internet Policy and Governance (pp. 3,5 and 6); the 2014 *Delhi Declaration for a Just and Equitable Internet*, the 2014 *Recommendation on a Guide to Human Rights for Internet Users* (p. 1), the 2014 *NETmundial Multistakeholder Statement* (pp. 6, 9 and 10), the 2014 *Paris Declaration* (p. 2), the 2014 released *EU Human Rights Guidelines on Freedom of Expression Online and Offline* (pp. 1 and 9), the 2014 Panel Report *Towards a Collaborative, Decentralized Internet Governance Ecosystem*, the 2014 *African Union Convention on Cyber Security and Personal Data Protection* (Article 27 No. 1 (b) (i)), the 2014 *Lyon Declaration on Access to Information and Development*, the 2014 *African Declaration on Internet Rights and Freedoms* and the 2014 United Nations *Resolution on the Right to Privacy in the Digital Age* (No. 4 [d]).

Only two documents thoroughly address accountability: (i) The Recommendation of the Council concerning Guidelines governing the Protection of Privacy and Transborder Flows of Personal Data, issued by the OECD Council on 11 July 2003, addresses specific issues of privacy and data protection; in this context, data controllers are obliged to implement accountability management programs. This development is of major importance, but it does not necessarily allow drawing conclusions by analogy for other Internet governance principles. (ii) The Report by the Panel on Global Internet Cooperation and Governance Mechanisms with the title *Towards a Collaborative, Decentralized Internet Governance Ecosystem* intensively looks at accountability issues. Topics addressed are the support for ICANN in its accountability improvement efforts, the development of a checklist on best practices for concepts of accountability in the multistakeholder model, the introduction of legal and political accountability for the protection of human rights, and the establishment of accountability proceedings within institutions (pp. 3, 23, 24, 33, 37, 38, 57 and 60).

From this analysis, the following conclusions can be drawn: (i) The proponents of the examined declarations, guidelines, and frameworks seem to have underestimated the value of internal accountability; this concept encompasses ex ante control, ongoing control and ex poste control. (ii) Furthermore, for informal cooperation to be effective in the long term, accountability is needed. Conversely, a core goal of accountability is the increase of effectiveness by learning from mistakes and feedback from stakeholders.[88] Accountability does not need to be understood (or be perceived) as polar opposite to effectiveness.

---

88   Weber, 2014, 80.

One positive accountability aspect of the last few years can be seen in the fact that an extended consultation of civil society as an actor in the preparation and development of documents as well as a (partly) improved inclusion of civil society in the decisionmaking processes have taken place. An example is the *NETmundial Multistakeholder Statement* of April 2014 which also reflects the input of civil society.

4.2 Salient Issues for UNESCO

The above summary of the findings derived from the analysis of more than 50 declarations, guidelines, and frameworks of Internet Governance principles can assist in clarifying salient issues for consideration in informing UNESCO action:

- As far as *freedom of expression and privacy* are concerned, many documents are available and the scope of coverage for these human rights is rather broad. This assessment does not mean that no further efforts are needed; UNESCO could become more active in respect of awareness raising and elaboration of existing principles. Their application to issues such as online safety, the confidentiality of journalists' sources, online hate speech, and media information literacy could thus be developed further. In addition, it is important to contribute to a broader recognition of these principles and promote their application.

- Technical and *economic openness* are important. Technical issues of open standards and open architectures could be largely left to the private experts, although there are also debates about governmental policy regulation in favour of network neutrality. But issues such as access to infrastructure and the openness of information and communication channels as well as public education resources could be improved with normative statements and policy elaboration by UNESCO working in conjunction with other UN actors.[89]

- The *social dimension of access* merits more attention; not only ethical issues (being partly mentioned in existing documents), but also issues of multilingualism and quality content as fostering of culture belong to the core objectives of UNESCO and could be strengthened in the future.

- A relatively strong movement towards *multistakeholder participation* can be observed for a few years. UNESCO is in a good position to further strengthen the understanding and practice related to multistakeholderism on Internet issues. Multistakeholder relations have a bearing on constructing knowledge societies. A good foundation has been laid with the NETmundial Declaration of Internet Governance Principles, but qualitative improvements by adding elaborated or additional principles are still possible.

- *Gender equality* has not yet become an important Internet Governance principle. However, especially since gender equality belongs to the priorities of UNESCO, efforts to elaborate this dimension in regard to Internet issues could be undertaken by the Organization.[90]

- *Sustainable development*, including the priority for Africa as a policy of UNESCO, remains an important goal that could be better implemented as a normative element of the Internet. Efforts in this direction could be combined with activity within the framework of the Sustainable Development Goals.

89　The Broadband Commission convened by UNESCO and the International Telecommunications Union is an example.
90　To the gender discussion in the UNESCO context see also MacKinnon et al., 2014, 169-178.

- *Ethical issues* although being a WSIS issue for attention have not yet gained a high level of attention in the reviewed documents. UNESCO is well suited to put more emphasis on ethical issues.[91] Such an initiative could be combined with other elements of the social dimension of access, particularly media and information literacy, multilingualism and quality content.

The "Universality Concept" underpins the fields of further activities identified in the UNESCO Internet Study, covering (i) access to information and knowledge, (ii) freedom of expression, (iii) privacy, (iv) and ethics. These fields can be mirrored against the four principles of rights, openness, accessibility, and multistakeholder participation. In so doing, the topics that merit particular attention can be reasonably identified. Based on this, templates and decision trees can be analytically developed. A first step into this direction has been done with the "Outcome document" as the closing document of the "CONNECTing the Dots: Options for Future Action" Conference held at UNESCO Headquarters on 3-4 March 2015.[92]

An important gap in the reviewed declarations, guidelines, and frameworks for Internet Governance principles consists in respect of accountability mechanisms. This lack has not so much an impact on the documents as such, but on the reality of implementing their principles.[93] In view of the reputation of UNESCO, principles affirmed, elaborated and developed by its Member States would have a fair chance to reach a high degree of global acceptance and implementation. UNESCO is institutionally in a good position to build bridges between diverse Internet Governance issues, as well as between different actors of manifold levels in this field. In this, the "Internet Universality" concept (the R.O.A.M. framework) can give UNESCO a strong identity in regard to what it stands for.

Furthermore, as noted by participants in the consultation in the Internet study, UNESCO could support the elaboration for consideration by Member States of implementation principles for taking forward Internet Governance in areas relevant to the mandate of the Organization. These could be translated as missions in the day-to-day activities of all stakeholders operating in the Internet. Amongst others, there is the idea of monitoring on an annual basis how the available Internet Governance principles are respected and implemented. By strengthening its own identity UNESCO could contribute to such activities.

5. Conclusions

The analysis of more than 50 declarations, guidelines, and frameworks containing Internet Governance principles in this study has been done in respect of the "Internet Universality" concept and the R.O.A.M framework as developed by UNESCO. In addition, the analysis has examined the range of documents from the point of view of UNESCO priorities and programmes.

In overview, the analysis enables the conclusion that manifold initiatives have been taken during the last 25 years. The prevailing impression remains that there is a diversity of documents and of attention to diverse Internet Governance principles. Patterns related to regions and stakeholders cannot be identified, because the contents of the assessed documents heavily depend on the given actors and environment at the time of the drafting. While a distributed ecology of declarations and principles does reflect the wide range of actors and issues concerned with the Internet, UNESCO itself is not particularly served by this situation.

---

91   See already "UNESCO and the Ethical Dimensions of the Information Society", endorsed by the Executive Board at its 190th session in 2012.
92   See <http://www.unesco.org/new/fileadmin/MULTIMEDIA/HQ/CI/CI/pdf/outcome_document.pdf>.
93   Accountability in the UNESCO context is also promoted by MacKinnon et al., 2014, 13 and 189/90.

While the normative character of the documents containing Internet Governance principles complements much of the mandate and work of UNESCO, there is no existing external document that covers all concerns of the Organization. Due to its cross-sectoral character, UNESCO is particularly well placed to advance universality in social inclusion, education, multilingualism, ethical thinking and gender equality.

With agreement of UNESCO Member States, the gap between existing statements and UNESCO's interests could be filled by the concept of "Internet Universality" and R.O.A.M framework, which provide a basis on which further issues important to the Organization can be elaborated. The R.O.A.M framework already encompasses the human rights pillar; the work by UNESCO concerning freedom of expression and the accessibility to information and knowledge is also relevant as well as the rights to education, equality, culture and development. These principles can be linked to communication and information issues, science, social and human science, as well as gender, Priority Africa, sustainable development, ethics, and other UNESCO concerns. Internet Universality and its principles might become a clear identifier of the Organization's way of approaching the various fields of Internet issues.[94]

As the Internet Universality concept and its principles are all at a general level, consensus amongst Member States on these and their relevance to UNESCO priorities may be achievable. Accountability for adopting such a broad position of principles relevant to the Internet is implied by UNESCO's structures and practices, which include the involvement of governments, National Commissions, and numerous civil society as well as private sector entities. Therefore, such principles have a very specific character, even if they could also prove to be of value to stakeholders outside of the Organization.

Due to its broad reach, UNESCO is also well placed to further develop indicators for R.O.A.M. This was a point made in several responses to the consultation for the UNESCO Internet Study. An example of indicators could be those for a successful multistakeholder process clarifying how meaningful participation is achieved and how stakeholders can reach the level of inclusiveness. Thereby, multistakeholderism could help process the real and potential conflicts that could otherwise fragment the Internet. The quality of multistakeholderism is essential for effectiveness and sustainability of Internet Governance.

If the normative and programmatic efforts of UNESCO are reinforced in this sense and if the "Internet Universality" is becoming more operational as outlined in this study, then policy development within each Member State can be enriched in line with the UNESCO mandate. In this way, UNESCO is able to contribute to a universal Internet that brings the sum of its Member States closer to being "Knowledge Societies".

The implementation of an online resource webpage (under UNESCO's website[95]) is a step toward mapping the field for further research. This more comprehensive online source can assist in overcoming the dispersed character of the existing documents, and in UNESCO's ongoing work in elaborating its positions on Internet-related issues within its mandate.

---

94 By comparison, the European Commission has an identifier summarised by the acronym C.O.M.P.A.C.T: "Internet as a space of Civic responsibilities, One unfragmented resource governed via a Multistakeholder approach to Promote democracy and human rights, based on a sound technological Architecture that engenders Confidence and facilitates a Transparent governance both of the underlying Internet infrastructure and of the services which run on top of it" (see European Commission, 2014).

95 http://www.unesco.org/new/en/communication-and-information/events/calendar-of-events/events-websites/connecting-the-dots/the-study/international-and-regional-instruments/.

6. References

Balleste, Roy, Internet Governance: Origins, Current Issues, and Future Possibilities, London 2015 (Balleste, 2015)

Benkler, Yochai, The Wealth of Networks: How Social Production Transforms Markets and Freedom, New Haven/London 2006 (Benkler, 2006)

Bygrave, Lee A., Data Privacy Law: An International Perspective, Oxford 2014 (Bygrave, 2014)

European Commission. Internet Policy and Governance: Europe's role in shaping the future of Internet Governance, Brussels, 2014 http://eur-lex.europa.eu/LexUriServ/LexUriServ.do?uri=COM:2014:0072:FIN:EN:PDF (European Commission 2014)

DeNardis, Laura, The Global War for Internet Governance, New Haven/London 2014 (DeNardis, 2014)

Jørgensen, Rikke Frank, Framing the Net: The Internet and Human Rights, Cheltenham 2013 (Jørgensen, 2013)

Lessig, Lawrence, Code and Other Laws of Cyberspace, New York 1999 (Lessig, 1999)

MacKinnon, Rebecca/Hickok, Elonnai/Bar, Allon/Lim, Hae-in, Fostering Freedom Online: The Role of Internet Intermediaries, UNESCO Series on Internet Freedom, Paris 2014 (MacKinnon et al., 2014)

Mueller, Milton, Networks and States: The Global Politics of Internet Governance, Cambridge MA 2010 (Mueller, 2010)

Weber, Rolf H., Shaping Internet Governance: Regulatory Challenges, Zurich 2009 (Weber, 2009)

Weber, Rolf H., Politics Through Social Networks and Politics by Government Blocking: Do We Need New Rules?, International Journal of Communication 2011, 1186-1194 (Weber, 2011)

Weber, Rolf H., Realizing a New Global Cyberspace Framework: Normative Foundations and Guiding Principles, Zurich/Basel/Geneva 2014 (Weber, 2014)

Weber, Rolf H./Heinrich, Ulrike I., Governance issues of the new media environment, in: Koltay, A. (ed.), Media Freedom and Regulation in the New Media World, Hungary 2014 (Weber/Heinrich, 2014)

Wilske, Stephan/Schiller, Teresa, International Jurisdiction in Cyberspace: Which States May Regulate the Internet?, Federal Communications Law Journal 1997, 50(1), Article 5, 117-178

WSIS, Tunis Agenda for the Information Society, World Summit on the Information Society, WSIS-05/TUNIS/DOC/6(Rev. 1)-E, 18 November 2005. Para 34. http://www.itu.int/wsis/docs2/tunis/off/6rev1.html

Appendix

Updated Version of UNESCO Discussion Paper (Summary version)

Internet Universality: A Means Towards Building Knowledge Societies and the Post-2015 Sustainable Development Agenda

2 September 2013

Abstract

UNESCO's Communication and Information Sector is canvassing a new concept of "Internet Universality", which could serve to highlight, holistically, the continued conditions for progress towards the Knowledge Society and the elaboration of the Post-2015 Sustainable Development Agenda. The concept includes, but also goes beyond, universal access to the Internet, mobile and ICTs. The word "Universality" points to four fundamental norms that have been embodied in the broad evolution of the Internet to date, and which provide a comprehensive way to understand how multiple different aspects are part of a wider whole. For the Internet to fulfill its historic potential, it needs to achieve fully-fledged "Universality" based upon the strength and interdependence of the following: (i) the norm that the Internet is Human Rights-based (which in this paper is the substantive meaning of a "free Internet"), (ii) the norm that it is "Open", (iii) the norm that highlights "Accessible to All", and (iv) the norm that it is nurtured by Multi-takeholder Participation. The four norms can be summarized by the mnemonic R – O – A – M (Rights, Openness, Accessibility, Multi-stakeholder). The "Internet Universality" concept has very specific value for UNESCO in particular. By building on UNESCO's existing positions on the Internet, the concept of "Internet Universality" can help frame much of UNESCO's Internet-related work in Education, Culture, Natural and Social Sciences and Communication-Information for the strategic period of 2014-2021. As regards global debates on Internet governance, the "Internet Universality" concept can help UNESCO facilitate international multi-stakeholder cooperation, and it can also help to highlight what the Organization can bring to the Post-2015 Sustainable Development Agenda.

By: Division of Freedom of Expression and Media Development

Communication and Information Sector[1]

Bommelaer for her contribution to the development of the concept.

* A full version of this paper in all UN official languages is online at http://www.unesco.org/new/en/communication-and-information/crosscutting-priorities/unesco-internetstudy/internet-universality/

---

1   This part of this book is compiled by UNESCO secretariat, not Prof Weber. The secretariat thanks Ms Constance Bommelaer for her contribution to the development of the concept of Internet Universality.

1. Why a concept of "Internet Universality"?

UNESCO has long recognized that the Internet has enormous potential to bring the world closer to peace, sustainable development and the eradication of poverty.[2] As an international intergovernmental organization that operates with a global remit and promotes values that are universal, UNESCO has a logical connection to the Internet's "universality". This "universality" can be understood as the common thread that runs through four key social dimensions pertaining to the Internet, namely the extent to which this facility is based on universal norms of being: (i) Human Rights-based (and therefore free); (ii) Open; (iii) Accessible to All; and (iv) Multi-stakeholder Participation. The four norms can be summarized by the mnemonic R– O – A – M (Rights, Openness, Accessibility, Multi-stakeholder).

Various stakeholders have characterized the Internet according to what they perceive as its essential features, highlighting one or other aspects such as freedom of expression, open architecture, security issues, online ethics, etc.[3]

What this range of conceptualisations illustrates is both the diversity of concerns and interests, as well as the multi-faceted character of the Internet itself. In turn, this prompts the question as to the possibility of understanding how the various considerations and dimensions relate to each other and to the wider whole. As a method to conceptualize this bigger picture, UNESCO is now canvassing the concept of "Internet Universality", which could serve as a macro-concept. The purpose is to capture the enduring essentials of the vast, complex and evolving Internet, and which facilitates a comprehensive understanding of where and how different parties, and especially UNESCO, relate to the Internet. The concept could particularly serve as an enabling perspective in the context of the increasing centrality of Internet to societies, and specifically the increasing "Internetization" of education, the sciences, culture and communication-information.

As well as identifying four distinctive norms that have special interest to UNESCO, the concept of "Internet Universality" groups these under a single integrated heading in a way that affords recognition of their mutually reinforcing and interdependent character. Without such a comprehensive intellectual device, it would otherwise be hard to grasp interconnections amongst UNESCO's Internet-related work and how it contributes to Knowledge Societies and the Post-2015 Sustainable Development Agenda.

As regards UNESCO's involvement in global debates, the concept of "Internet Universality" can be considered for its potential as a unifying, consolidated and comprehensive framework. On the one hand, it highlights the freedom and human rights principles as shared by those existing notions such as "Internet freedom"; on the other hand, it also provides an umbrella to address the intertwined issues of access and use, as well as the matters of technical and economic openness. In addition, the concept also encompasses

---

2 For example: "Reflection and Analysis by UNESCO on the Internet: UNESCO and the use of Internet in its domains of competence" (2011). http://www.unesco.org/new/fileadmin/MULTIMEDIA/HQ/ED/ICT/pdf/useinternetdomains.pdf

3 For example, there have been different emphases at the Stockholm Forum, the Freedom Online Coalition on Cyberspace, Wilton Park, and the London and Budapest conferences on Cyberspace. Similarly, the Internet has been analyzed diversely by international organisations. Examples here are: the Council of Europe's "Recommendation CM/Rec(2011)8 of the Committee of Ministers to member states on the protection and promotion of the universality, integrity and openness of the Internet" (2011), the OECD Council Recommendation on Principles for Internet Policy Making (2011), the OSCE Representative on Freedom of the Media Recommendations from the Internet 2013 Conference (2013); the ICC Policy Statement on "The freedom of expression and the free flow of information on the Internet", and the Internet Rights and Principles Coalition's "Internet Rights & Principles Charter" (2010).

multi-stakeholder engagement as an integral component. In this inclusive way, the "Internet Universality" concept can therefore be a bridging and foresighted framework for dialogue between North and South and among different stakeholders. As such, it could also make a unique contribution to shaping global Internet governance discourse and the post-2015 Sustainable Development Agenda.

2. Unpacking the concept of "Internet Universality"

The linking of four normative components of the "universality" of the Internet builds closely upon prior UNESCO thinking about the Internet which includes:

- Recommendation on the Promotion and Use of Multilingualism and Universal Access to Cyberspace (2003).[4] (This document particularly points to the accessibility norm, as well as the need to balance rights).

- Reflection and Analysis by UNESCO on the Internet (2011).[5] (This document highlights normative work in relation to UNESCO's programmes, and multi-stakeholder participation).

- Final Recommendations of WSIS+10 review event, and the Final Statement of the WSIS+10 review event (2013).[6] (These cover rights, access, openness, and multi-stakeholder issues).

- UNGIS (UN Group on the Information Society) Joint Statement on the Post-2015 Sustainable Development Agenda (2013).[7] (This document highlights the importance of the social conditions for Information and Communication Technologies in general, and the Internet in particular, to contribute to inclusive Knowledge Societies).

"Internet Universality" integrates a range of existing UNESCO insights and shows the link between the Internet and what UNESCO has already recognised[8] as the underlying key principles of Knowledge Societies: freedom of expression, quality education for all, universal access to information and knowledge, and respect for cultural and linguistic diversity. In this way, the concept highlights what is needed for the Internet to be a means towards achieving Knowledge Societies. It serves as a heuristic to highlight that the Internet's character and utility entail technical, social, legal, economic and other arrangements which in turn depend on particular norms that underpin the positive potentiality of this facility. Considered in more depth, the R – O – A – M norms constitutive of "Internet Universality" (Rights, Openness, Accessibility, Multi-stakeholder) can be understood as follows:

(i) By identifying the Internet's connection to Human Rights-based norms as constituents of freedom, "Internet Universality" helps to emphasize continued harmony between

---

4 http://www.unesco.org/new/en/communication-and-information/about-us/how-we-work/strategy-and-programme/promotion-and-use-of-multilingualism-and-universal-access-to-cyberspace/
5 http://unesdoc.unesco.org/images/0019/001920/192096e.pdf;
6 Documents from the First WSIS+10 Review Event, "Towards Knowledge Societies for Peace and Sustainable Development", Paris 25-27 February, 2013: http://www.unesco.org/new/fileadmin/MULTIMEDIA/HQ/CI/CI/pdf/wsis/WSIS_10_Event/wsis10_recommendations_en.pdf; http://www.unesco.org/new/fileadmin/MULTIMEDIA/HQ/CI/CI/pdf/wsis/WSIS_10_Event/wsis10_final_statement_en.pdf
7 http://www.unesco.org/new/fileadmin/MULTIMEDIA/HQ/CI/CI/pdf/wsis/ungis_joint_statement_wsis_2013.pdf
8 Reflection and Analysis by UNESCO on the Internet, http://unesdoc.unesco.org/images/0019/001920/192096e.pdf

the growth and use of the Internet and human rights. A free Internet in this sense means one that respects and enables the freedom to exercise human rights.[9] In this regard, "Internet Universality" enjoins us to consider the gamut of interdependencies and inter-relationships between different human rights and the Internet – such as freedom of expression, privacy, cultural participation, gender equality, association, security, education, etc.

(ii) "Internet Universality" also highlights the norm of the Internet being Open. This designation recognizes the importance of technological issues such as open standards, as well as standards of open access to knowledge and information. Openness also signals the importance of ease of entry of actors and the absence of closure that might otherwise be imposed through monopolies.

(iii) Accessible to All as a norm for "Internet Universality" raises issues of technical access and availability, as well as digital divides such as based on economic income and urban-rural inequalities. Thus it points to the importance of norms around universal access to minimum levels of connectivity infrastructure. At the same time, "accessibility" requires engaging with social exclusions from the Internet based on factors such as literacy, language, class, gender, and disability. Further, understanding that people access the Internet as producers of content, code and applications, and not just as consumers of information and services, the issue of user competencies is part of the accessibility dimension of "Universality". This highlights UNESCO's notion of Media and Information Literacy which enhances accessibility by empowering Internet users to engage critically, competently and ethically.

(iv) The Internet in this sense cannot only be seen from the "supply side", but needs a complimentary "user-centric" perspective. The Participatory, and specifically the Multi-stakeholder engagement, dimension of "Internet Universality" facilitates sense-making of the roles that different agents (representing different sectors as well as different social and economic status, and not excluding women and girls) have played, and need to continue to play, in developing and governing the Internet on a range of levels. Participation is essential to the value that the facility can have for peace, sustainable development and poverty eradication. In bridging contesting stakeholder interests, participative mechanisms contribute to shared norms that mitigate abuses of the Internet. "Universality" here highlights shared governance of the Internet.

These norms for these four aspects are distinct, but they also reinforce each other. Rights without accessibility would be limited to the few; accessibility without rights would stunt the potential of access. Openness allows for sharing and innovation, and it complements respect for rights and accessibility. Multi-stakeholder participation helps guarantee the other three norms. Overall, an Internet that falls short of respecting human rights, openness, accessibility or multi-stakeholder participation would by definition be far less than universal.

---

9   In this manner, "Internet Universality" accords with the Report of UN Special Rapporteur on the promotion and protection of the right to freedom of opinion and expression and also echoes the first resolution on "promotion, protection and enjoyment of human rights on the Internet" passed by UN Human Rights Council in 2012.

3. How the concept of "Internet Universality" is relevant to UNESCO

UNESCO has a unique role in promoting "Internet Universality". It is the UN agency with a mandate that spans social life at large and, within this, has programs that involve the Internet in education, culture, science, social sciences and communication-information. By using "Internet Universality" as an umbrella concept, UNESCO can position more specific concerns such as mobile learning, education for girls, cultural and linguistic diversity, media and information literacy, research into climate change, freedom of expression, universal access to information, bioethics and social inclusion, etc. In this way, "Internet Universality" can also support the priorities of Gender Equality and Africa. It can serve as an over-arching, integrating framework for Internet-related work across UNESCO, establishing a common frame of reference for all. Operationally the concept can elevate a range of work to the status of initiatives that jointly advance "Internet Universality". It can encourage synergies and intersectoral co-operation and joint programming. In particular, the concept can enhance understanding of the mid-term strategy of 2014-2021 (37/C4) and the quadrennial program (37/C5).-

4. Conclusion

"Internet Universality" accords with the Organization's service to the wider international community in the following respects:

- Laboratory of ideas, including foresight – elaborating the concept is directly relevant to UNESCO's creative and think-tank potential;

- By stimulating global debate, "Internet Universality" illustrates how UNESCO can be a catalyst for international cooperation, with a holistic and inclusive approach.

- Standard-setter – if the concept gained traction broadly, it could inform the development of standards for monitoring progress in "Internet Universality"

- As a normative framework that can inform policies, and draw in public and private, civil society and decision-makers, "Internet Universality" can help UNESCO fulfill its role as a capacity-builder in Member States.

Looking ahead, "Internet Universality" could follow in the footsteps of previous influential intellectual work by UNESCO such as the concepts of "Intangible cultural heritage" and "Knowledge Societies". Because "Internet Universality" represents an updated conceptualization of the era, the concept could become a valuable contribution to the global discussion about this complex and dynamic human creation and serve to enhance Internet's continued contribution to humanity's shared future.